Occasional Paper Series | **11**

Terrorism and International Cooperation

Martha Crenshaw

 **Institute for East-West Security Studies**
New York 1989

The Institute for East-West Security Studies does not take or encourage specific policy positions. It is committed to encouraging and facilitating discussions of important issues of concern to East and West. The views expressed in this book do not necessarily reflect the opinions of the Board of Directors, the officers or the staff of the Institute.

This publication is made possible through the generous support of the Ploughshares Fund of San Francisco, the Ford Foundation and John D. and Catherine T. MacArthur Foundation.

Distributed by Westview Press
   Frederick A. Praeger, Publisher
   5500 Central Avenue
   Boulder, Colorado 80301

Library of Congress Cataloging-in-Publication Data

Crenshaw, Martha.
   Terrorism and international cooperation/by Martha Crenshaw.
      p. cm.
   ISBN 0-913449-11-3 (Institute): $7.95.—ISBN 0-8133-7797-8 (Westview)
   1. Terrorism.. 2. Terrorism—Prevention—International cooperation. I. Title.
   HV6431.C76   1989
   363.3'2—dc20   89-2132
                                                                 CIP

Printed in the United States of America

TABLE OF CONTENTS

It was not long ago that terrorism was considered a Western problem and a major obstacle to improving relations between the United States and the Soviet Union as well as between East and West. There was no consensus on what constituted a terrorist act and no acceptance of the proposition that East and West could seriously discuss cooperation in fighting terrorism.

The issue looks quite different in 1989. Despite strong skepticism in some quarters, prominent officials in Moscow and Washington have issued public proposals calling for discussions on possible East-West cooperation in combatting terrorism. Joint efforts against terrorism are being labeled potential confidence-building measures in East-West relations. It is now widely accepted that terrorism increasingly threatens the East as well as the West and that the potentially destabilizing effects of terrorism have the capacity to severely aggravate existing strains in the international order and undermine the continued improvement of East-West relations.

Terrorism causes alarm because it appears contagious across nations and regions and has spilled over from domestic arenas of conflict into world politics, threatening international commerce and diplomacy and frequently involving attacks on victims with no responsibility for the conditions supposed to motivate or justify violence. The issue of terrorism raises deep and troubling questions about the permissibility, effectiveness and limits of civil violence. It has caused a widening of divisions and suspicions between East and West, between North and South and between the United States and its NATO allies. As such, terrorism is a common problem which needs to be dealt with effectively and on a cooperative basis whenever possible. Unilateral responses to terrorism have proved insufficient. The changing international environment makes multilateral cooperation in fighting terrorism both more necessary and possible.

In this study Martha Crenshaw, Professor of Government at Wesleyan University and a 1987–1988 American Scholar-in-Residence at the Institute for East-West Security Studies, provides a thoroughly readable assessment of the nature of terrorism and the possibilities and conditions for international cooperation in combatting it. A former advisor on terrorism to the U.S. secretary of state, Dr. Crenshaw deals with an aspect of cooperation that until recently would have been considered highly controversial, if not unthinkable—the possibility of East-West cooperation against terrorism. She concludes that such a possibility exists and that, in fact, there already is significant ongoing East-West cooperation to prevent terrorists from acquiring nuclear devices. She considers that under General Secretary Mikhail Gorbachev, a Soviet interest in pursuing cooperative measures has been expressed with some insistence, and that the United States could benefit from this apparent change of attitude. Under the Bush administration, the issue of possible cooperation in combatting terrorism has in effect been placed on the agenda for East-West talks.

Dr. Crenshaw calls for the development of a pragmatic approach to countering terrorism, based on an objective definition of the threat and realistic analysis of the wider political context within which it occurs. She recommends the isolation of terrorism as unacceptable regardless of its political motivation, and that cooperation in the battle against terrorism should be rewarded and noncooperation punished. Dr. Crenshaw warns against inflated expectations of the immediate gains from international cooperation in combatting terrorism. Terrorism can be reduced but not eradicated. Progress is likely to be incremental rather than comprehensive, and national efforts from all sides must be based on recognition of the difficulties inherent in dealing with a highly complex and troublesome political problem that is too often oversimplified.

Martha Crenshaw wrote this study while an American Scholar-in-Residence at the Institute for East-West Security

Studies in New York during 1987–1988. The study was exposed to the critical review of the Institute's 1987–1988 Fellows research team, which was composed of security specialists from Eastern and Western Europe and the United States. The author would like to thank the 1987–1988 Fellows as well as the academic staff of the Institute, including in particular Vice President and Director of Studies F. Stephen Larrabee, Deputy Director of Studies Allen Lynch and Research Associate Ian Cuthbertson, for their valuable comments and critiques. She would also like to thank Institute Director of Publications Peter B. Kaufman and Publications Editor Mary Albon for devoting much time and effort to guiding the manuscript through all stages of production.

The author's fellowship at the Institute was made possible by the generous support of the Ploughshares Fund of San Francisco. The Institute also gratefully acknowledges the funding of the Ford Foundation and the John D. and Catherine T. MacArthur Foundation for the publication and distribution of this Occasional Paper. The views in this study are solely those of its author and should not be ascribed to the Institute or its funders. The Institute for East-West Security Studies is pleased to sponsor the publication of this Occasional Paper on a subject that could become a confidence-building effort between East and West rather than remaining a destabilizing and negative force as in the past.

John Edwin Mroz
President
April 1989

1
Introduction

The American foreign policy community is actively engaged in a review of U.S. diplomacy toward the Soviet Union, a reaction to Soviet "new thinking" as well as to the opportunities for new American foreign policy initiatives that coincide with presidential election years. The idea that terrorism might be an area of possible cooperation between East and West at first seems unlikely, given the propensity of both sides to use the term as a label for condemning the policies of the other. However, the issue has been raised as a potentially fruitful topic for East-West dialogue not only by the Institute for East-West Security Studies but by other knowledgeable observers. For example, Zbigniew Brzezinski, speaking to the Trilateral Commission in 1986, recommended that terrorism be placed on the East-West agenda because of its potential for creating discord in the Western alliance. According to Brzezinski, not present changes in the Soviet outlook but past Soviet responsibility for embracing terrorism as a form of strategically beneficial disruption in the 1970s makes it important to include the issue in joint discussions. He urged the United States to move beyond the "simplistic activism" of past anti-terrorism policy, to recognize the complexity of its multiple layers of activities, but not acquiesce to the passivity of the West Europeans.[1] Similarly, Dimitri K. Simes and Keith Bickel recently suggested a Washington-Moscow anti-terrorism agreement. Their position is that preventing Soviet exploitation of regional disputes is a key American interest, and that

---

1. Report on the Madrid Plenary meeting of The Trilateral Commission, May 1986, p. 42. Available from The Trilateral Commission, New York.

"While no comprehensive code of conduct concerning the Third World is feasible, Washington might benefit from inviting Moscow to sign a tightly formulated anti-terrorism agreement barring military aid to nations and movements that target innocent civilians."[2] In addition, in January 1989 private American foreign policy specialists met with several Soviet counterparts in Moscow to recommend common measures against terrorism.

The purpose of this paper is to examine the possibility of East-West cooperation against terrorism. It looks first at the nature of terrorism and, in examining the background to the issue, questions some of the assumptions on which past American policy has been based. It then assesses the status of international cooperation and the prospects for American-Soviet agreement. International arrangements to prevent nuclear terrorism are already under way, and they may be considered a model for future cooperation. In general, the incentives for cooperation can outweigh the disadvantages if the United States is willing to adopt a pragmatic and realistic policy. It is imperative that rhetoric and actions be brought into balance.

Twenty years ago the phenomenon of political terrorism was not considered an issue of international security. It became so as acts of terrorism transcended the borders of national territories under dispute and targeted civilians who could not be considered legitimate victims by any standards of warfare. It seemed to be a bizarre form of warfare occurring in peacetime. The logic of the issue of international terrorism—a type of violence that preys on international commerce, communications, and diplomacy—has persuaded many that international cooperation is the most appropriate method of prevention and control, far preferable to unilateral action. Yet implementing cooperative measures has proved difficult. Accurately specifying the problem that is to be solved is a necessary first step, but the effort to define terrorism has led to widespread confusion and misunderstanding. Definitions are often subjective and self-serving, or thought to be so by those who oppose the political interpretation they support. The international community is still working to develop a common and acceptable

---

2. "For Fresh Diplomacy Toward Moscow," *The New York Times*, April 1, 1988.

vocabulary for discussing the issue. Some ambiguities are unavoidable because they stem from the fact that terrorism is a complex and diverse activity, assuming a variety of forms, including hostage-taking, mass-casualty bombings, assassinations and hijackings, and claiming a variety of motives, some comprehensible and some manifestly unrealistic. To pretend that terrorism is a unitary phenomenon is a misleading oversimplification, although terrorist activity has patterns and structures.

2

The Nature of the Problem

■ Defining Terrorism

The term terrorism has acquired a pejorative connotation, not only as governments use it but also as revolutionaries or nationalists use it, although this negative usage has not always been the case.[3] The word has become a political label rather than an analytical concept, used to condemn one's enemies rather than to specify what terrorism is and what it is not. Terrorism is irreversibly linked to questions of legitimacy in international as well as domestic politics. Although it is theoretically possible to consider terrorism solely as a method or strategy of opposition, in practice the condemnation of terrorism as a means is often interpreted as an implicit disavowal of the ends it serves. Whatever the intended meaning, in asserting that an action in question is terrorism, one is understood as communicating opposition to its objectives. Emotional associations are unavoidable in using the terms of ordinary political discourse, such as aggression, imperialism, racism or terrorism. It would be naive to pretend that terrorism is an innocuous term. But ends must be separated from means in politics.

In defining the concept of terrorism for purposes of analysis it is critical to isolate terrorism from specific political goals; that is, all nationalists, revolutionaries or far-right

---

3. The history of the word shows that in the nineteenth century revolutionaries were proud to call themselves terrorists. Since World War II it has become a term of opprobrium that is rejected for more neutral descriptions such as "urban guerrilla warfare." However, Carlos Marighela referred explicitly to terrorism as a part of urban guerrilla warfare in *For the Liberation of Brazil* (Harmondsworth: Penguin, 1971).

extremists are not terrorists. No particular ideology or religion is responsible for terrorism. Terrorism as a means is logically separable from the ends it purportedly serves. Terrorist behavior can be distinguished from its causes in order to control it. This approach has been necessary to the formulation of international law on the subject, which has focused on the component parts of terrorism, such as hijackings or diplomatic kidnappings, in order to treat them as crimes.

If one accepts that terrorism is a specific and identifiable type of political violence, then its attributes must be listed. It is organized and purposive activity, not a spontaneous reaction to circumstances. Terrorism involves violence perceived as unacceptable by society because of its cruelty and unexpectedness. The form of violence itself may be horrifying, such as mid-air explosions of airliners or kidnappings. Terrorism usually occurs in situations of peace rather than war, and comes as a surprise to its victims. A particularly salient characteristic of this form of violence is the usual innocence of its victims, who are noncombatants, not prepared to defend themselves against attack and only in the most tenuous way responsible for the actions of the governments that terrorists oppose. The victims of terrorism are often those who bear the least offensive intentions toward the terrorists—airline passengers, journalists, diplomats, educators, business executives and other civilians. Random assaults on civilian populations are not a new form of terrorism; the anarchists and Irish nationalists of the nineteenth century threw bombs into crowded restaurants or concealed them in subways or train stations. Modern terrorists are more likely to choose this tactic rather than the traditional reliance on assassinations of heads of state or prominent officials, who are now well-protected. Terrorists prefer easy targets. Yet the technical destructiveness of modern terrorism—the capacity to explode bombs of sufficient force to kill hundreds of people—appears to coincide with a lessening of moral inhibitions about the use of violence. This erosion of inhibitions may be due in part to the actions of states whose brutalities against their own citizens in peacetime and use of strategic bombing of cities in wartime set an example of disregard for innocent lives. Yet somehow the psychological effects of oppositional terrorism are more shocking to world sensibilities.

Terrorism is also distinguished by secrecy. Its perpetrators are anonymous, their identities deliberately concealed behind facades of ordinariness or actual masks. Their violence is unexpected and frightening not only because it violates conventional expectations of behavior but because their preparations are clandestine. Terrorists are not easily recognizable as enemies. Thus terrorism can be considered a form of deception.

Terrorism is often referred to as the weapon of the weak, since it is frequently the resort of small ideological groups that lack a mass base. It is often a substitute for the mobilization of large numbers of supporters. However, terrorist tactics can accompany large-scale national liberation movements. The Algerian FLN was responsible for the 1956–1957 campaign of bombings of European civilians in Algiers, which together with the severely repressive French response constituted the "Battle of Algiers," subsequently dramatized in a popular film directed by Gillo Pontecorvo. In turn, elements from the French military and the settler population of Algeria formed the terrorist "Secret Army Organization" to stop the movement toward independence.

These features of terrorism lead analysts to infer that terrorists intend, if not to terrorize (that is, to create the emotion of terror, a form of panic), at least to produce outrage and shock. Terrorism is a strategy of surprise. It is meant to be an economical method, in the sense of producing psychological and political effects far out of proportion to the magnitude of physical destruction. What is characteristic of terrorism is that the physical victims of terrorism are not the targets. That they are terrorized is important only in so far as their terror is communicated to a watching audience, whose emotions the terrorists seek to manipulate. If this audience is sufficiently stimulated to support or agree to the terrorists' demands, then terrorism has succeeded. Such a response, however, is rare. It is important to note that the relevant audiences for terrorism extend beyond the citizens of the country the terrorists oppose. Potential supporters are also a critical audience, and terrorism serves as a useful device for both mobilization and polarization of populations. It is a way of forcing people to choose sides. Terrorism thus has diverse emotional effects: it can arouse enthusiasm, satisfy desires for vengeance or stimulate imitation. The importance of publicity to transmitting the appropriate message to audiences is undeniable, but it is not likely that the news media provide a faithful representation of the terrorist cause. Distortion of the message the terrorists intend is an impediment to its effectiveness. It seems unlikely that the immediate emotional effects of violence can easily be converted into influence over long-term outcomes.

Terrorism is often confused with guerrilla warfare, since both activities involve low-level violence (in terms of physical destructiveness) by weaker parties in conflicts. Both are convenient methods for challenging the power of the state. The rise of the concept of "urban guerrilla warfare" in Latin America in the 1960s further confuses the issue. Difficulties in distinguishing between the two are naturally compounded when Third World nationalist or revolutionary movements, with claims to substantial popular support or control of territory, use methods that are essentially terrorist. There is a tendency to type all users of terrorism as "terrorist organizations," as, for example, in the Israeli attitude toward the PLO. However, such a label seems to be a misnomer when applied to groups that do not rely exclusively on terrorism, for which in effect terrorism may be a quite peripheral tactic.

A further problem is that in civil conflicts the distinction between combatants and noncombatants is blurred. Attempts to define terrorism are in many ways efforts to uphold that distinction. If terrorism is to be regarded as unacceptable violence, then the rules for what is acceptable violence must be established. Guerrilla warfare is conventionally thought of as violence against military targets primarily for military effect, although it necessarily avoids prolonged engagements with a more powerful government force. Its primary objectives are to seize territory and control populations, neither of which is a primary goal of terrorism.

Terrorism that qualifies as international or transnational involves actions in which the nationality of the victims is different from that of the perpetrator, or the operation is extraterritorial, located outside the boundaries of a contested area. The U.S. State Department defines terrorism as "premeditated, politically motivated violence perpetrated against noncombatant targets by subnational groups or clandestine state agents, usually intended to influence an audience." To be international, it must involve the citizens or territory of more than one country.[4] Such terrorism strongly reflects the interdependence of the international system. It would not be possible if nations were not linked in complex networks of mutual political and economic interests. Were there no tourists, no diplomats and no business travellers, terrorism could not have assumed the forms it has. International terrorism has been characterized most notably by attacks on diplomats or diplomatic facilities, on civil aviation (aircraft and airports) and on foreign businessmen, journalists and educators. Its second important characteristic is the seizure of hostages in order to bargain with their governments or with the host government where the kidnapping or barricade occurs. Terrorism has become a modern form of coercive bargaining, in which the terrorists have the initiative. Their demands usually include the release of prisoners, the payment of a monetary ransom, or the publication of a communication. The inherent drama of hostage seizures, particularly barricade incidents, such as the takeover of the Dominican Republic Embassy in Colombia or the Saudi Arabian Embassy in Khartoum, as well as the concern of governments for their citizens and for their international reputation, exacerbate the issue of whether or not concessions should be made to terrorist demands. The current situation in Lebanon has highlighted this policy dilemma.

■ Sources of Contemporary Terrorism

The historical manifestations of terrorism are diverse and complex. The academic community has yet to achieve an intellectual understanding of why terrorism happens, the forms it takes or how it ends. Neither the causes nor the consequences of terrorism can be satisfactorily explained. Nevertheless, finding an appropriate policy response to terrorism on both national and international levels depends on such understanding. The need for objective inquiry into the evolution of terrorism is essential both for the development of coordinated policies and for public understanding of the nature of the threat and of the feasibility and legitimacy of government actions in response. It is imperative that stereotypes and misconceptions about terrorism be replaced by a

---

4. U.S. Department of State, Office of the Ambassador at Large for Counter-Terrorism, *Patterns of Global Terrorism: 1986* (Washington, DC: 1988).

sophisticated appreciation of its ramifications. Treatment of the issue must rise above polemical debates.

An interpretation that gained popularity in the United States during the 1980s holds that terrorism primarily reflects conflict between the United States and the Soviet Union or world communism.[5] The proponents of this view argue that ideological affinity motivates radical non-state organizations to act as the pliant accomplices of enemy states, including Iran and Libya as well as the Soviet Union. To this school of thought, terrorist organizations and their government supporters are linked in a global network, so that all incidents of terrorism, however disparate, are actually manifestations of the same malicious intent. Terrorism is perceived as a potent yet widely ignored threat to the internal stability and foreign interests of Western democracies. This "Cold War" view finds that terrorism has become an attractive strategy for the actors in international politics, preferable to conventional or nuclear warfare, which have become too risky and too expensive, and that its use by hostile states gives terrorism the potential to alter the international balance of power. This position leads to advocacy of a tougher response to terrorism and the accusation that the leaders of Western democracies are blind to the threat, lacking in resolve, confused, weak and vacillating. Its implication is that terrorism is a problem caused by states, not by dissident undergrounds with agendas of their own. Terrorist organizations are denied any autonomy. The threat of terrorism is thus elevated to a position of high significance for national security.

However, in reality there is no monolithic terrorist entity. Instead terrorism appears highly eclectic and pluralistic. In 1985, over sixty different organizations were noted as engaged in international terrorism. Fifty were counted in 1986 and

---

5. These works include several by Ray S. Cline and Yonah Alexander: *Terrorism: The Soviet Connection* (New York: Crane, Russak, 1984); *Terrorism as State-Sponsored Covert Warfare: What the Free World Must Do To Protect Itself* (Fairfax, VA: HERO Books, 1986); and the Report for the Subcommittee on Security and Terrorism of the Committee on the Judiciary, U.S. Senate, *State-Sponsored Terrorism* (1985). See also *Hydra of Carnage: International Linkages of Terrorism,* edited by Uri Ra'anan, Robert L. Pfaltzgraff, Richard H. Shultz, Jr., Ernst Halperin, and Igor Lukes (Lexington, MA: Lexington Books, 1986).

fifty-six in 1987.[6] The major perpetrators of acts of international terrorism account for roughly half of all incidents, which shows that the distribution of responsibility for terrorism is broad. The highest ranking group, the Islamic Jihad, accounted for only 8.6 percent of all incidents in 1985. In 1986, the MRTA (Tupac Amaru Revolutionary Movement) in Peru led with 6.6 percent followed closely by the Colombian ELN (National Liberation Army) and the Lebanese Armed Revolutionary Factions, each with 6.2 percent. In general, Middle Eastern terrorism, whether Palestinian or Lebanese, accounts for over half of all international terrorist incidents, which in 1985 spilled over into Western Europe. In 1985, eighty-four countries were victimized by international terrorism; in 1986, the number was seventy-eight.

The alliances among these organizations are tenuous. A recent study of transnational terrorism concludes that coalitions among groups are infrequent, ad hoc and short in duration.[7] The commonality of interests among terrorist organizations does not seem sufficient to sustain long-term operational coordination, although the fact of transient linkages is undeniable. In 1987, the "Anti-Imperialist International Brigades," thought to be an alliance of the Popular Front for the Liberation of Palestine and the Japanese Red Army, carried out four relatively amateurish attacks against Western targets, including the Venice summit meeting. In 1972, however, their cooperation produced deadly results when an attack on an arriving Air France flight at Israel's Lod airport left twenty-eight dead and seventy-six wounded.

An important reason for the conclusion that terrorism threatens international security is the charge of state sponsorship. Many observers think that terrorism is likely to become a form of surrogate warfare, employed equally by nonstates and by states too weak to mount a conventional military challenge. In 1985, the U.S. Department of State considered twelve per-

---

6. These statistics come from *InTer 85: A Review of International Terrorism in 1985*, and similarly for 1986 and 1987, published by the *Jerusalem Post* and the Jaffee Center for Strategic Studies of Tel Aviv University. See also the State Department annual reports on terrorism cited above.
7. Kent Layne Oots, *A Political Organization Approach to Transnational Terrorism* (Westport, CT: Greenwood Press, 1986), pp. 132–133.

cent of international terrorist incidents to be state-supported, the majority by Middle Eastern governments. State support was thought to be linked to the increasing destructiveness of terrorism, which in 1984 killed 20 percent more people than the average of the preceding four years. The British strategic theorist Lawrence Freedman agrees that state sponsorship challenges international security, but warns that the need to justify policies of military retaliation is likely to lead to an exaggeration of this threat.[8]

The precise relationship between states and terrorist undergrounds is difficult to determine. Some states have provided the financial and logistical support that has made international terrorism possible, but whether the dependency relationships thus created entail state *control* over the actions of such groups is hard to know. Iran seems to influence but not determine the fate of foreign hostages held by Hezbollah in Lebanon. Linkages between states and undergrounds are not uncommon, although they only came to the attention of Western governments in the 1980s. Since 1967, Arab states have maintained affiliations with various Palestinian factions, some of them responsible for terrorism. Syria has long been linked to the Popular Front for the Liberation of Palestine-General Command. Libya is connected to Abu Nidal's anti-PLO group, the Fatah Revolutionary Council. Reliance on proxies seems to be favored over the direct use of government agents, but both practices are familiar in the Middle East.

Scholars disagree as to whether the terrorism that plagues the world community results from the extraterritorial spillover of local grievances or whether it is a deliberate attack on international order. The effects of terrorism on international security may be incidental to its intended impact on the local distribution of power. For example, the conflict between Israel and Palestinian Arabs over who is to rule the territory that was formerly the Palestine Mandate is at the root of much of the anti-American violence that has made terrorism salient to the U.S. government. The Palestinian factions that practice terrorism outside of Israel (and it is mistaken to equate the PLO with

---

8. Lawrence Freedman, "Terrorism and Strategy," in Lawrence Freedman, et al., *Terrorism and International Order* (London: Routledge & Kegan Paul, 1986. Chatham House Special Paper.)

all Palestinian radicalism) seek not to upset the international balance of power but to compel Israel to surrender to their demands for a secular Palestine with an Arab majority. Because the United States is seen, not unreasonably, as Israel's chief ally, the change in American policy toward the PLO will affect a wide range of relationships.

In the 1970s when diplomatic kidnappings were fashionable in Latin America, the intent of groups such as the Tupamaros of Uruguay or Carlos Marighela's Brazilian Action for National Liberation was to seize power at home. They sought to compel an American withdrawal as a prerequisite for domestic revolution because they attributed the strength of the regimes they opposed to military and economic assistance supplied by the United States.[9]

In contrast, however, terrorism sponsored by Iran or pro-Iranian factions in Lebanon and Kuwait is directed toward changing the regional balance of power and driving outside interests from the Middle East. Its aims are clearly international, going far beyond the issue of who governs Lebanon. Kidnappings of French nationals, for example, were considered to be related to French support for Iraq during the Iran-Iraq war as well as to debts owned to Iran by France.

International terrorism is a major concern of the world community, but by no means do all groups operate outside their borders or resort to hijacking airliners or attacking foreign diplomats. The Basque ETA and the IRA, for example, generally confine their actions to the domestic arena of conflict (which for the IRA includes Great Britain and the Republic of Ireland). So, too, do Tamil separatists in Sri Lanka and the African National Congress in South Africa. Sendero Luminoso of Peru is the most serious terrorist organization operating in Latin America today, yet it is extremely parochial. However, as the interests of such groups shift, so do their targets. ETA, for example, has begun to attack French targets because of the French decision to extradite ETA members to Spain. Sendero Luminoso, which follows a Maoist orientation, bombed the

---

9. Marighela's work (fn. 3) remains instructive on strategies of oppositional terrorism in Latin America. See also Carol Edler Baumann, *The Diplomatic Kidnappings: A Revolutionary Tactic of Urban Terrorism* (The Hague: Nijhoff, 1973).

Soviet Embassy in Lima in 1986. Sikh separatists and Armenian terrorists have local aims but act on the international scene. International terrorism represents a type of strategy, not a type of terrorism.

■ The Role of Ideology

In describing the diversity of terrorism, it is important to stress that not all groups that employ terrorism claim an affiliation with ideologies of the revolutionary left or nationalism. In the 1980s neo-Fascist terrorism erupted in West Germany, France and Italy.[10] High-casualty bombings at the Bologna railroad station, the Munich Oktoberfest and a Paris synagogue signalled this development. There appears to be a loose relationship among different European groups, as well as between the West German Hoffmann Military Sports Group and Middle Eastern organizations (the Lebanese phalange and the PLO) and between European groups and American extremists such as the Ku Klux Klan, Posse Comitatus or The Order, which is a faction of the Aryan Nations, founded in 1983 to overthrow the U.S. government. Posse Comitatus, founded in 1969, is a tax protest group that has become increasingly violent.

From an analytical as opposed to a political perspective, ideology is often neglected as a motivating factor for terrorism because the professed beliefs of some groups, especially the terrorist undergrounds in Western Europe, often appear confused and inconsistent. Certainly adherence to a given ideology does not dictate the resort to terrorism. Furthermore, the priority of terrorists is action rather than thinking. To Carlos Marighela, who left the Brazilian Communist Party to form an underground movement, action creates the vanguard.[11] In fact, many recruits into terrorist organizations left political parties or protest movements because there was too much discussion and not enough action. Yet it is important to take into account the meaning terrorists themselves ascribe to their actions and

---

10. See Bruce Hoffman, *Right-Wing Terrorism in Europe*, Rand Note 1856-AF (Santa Monica: The Rand Corporation, 1982). See also Paul Wilkinson, *The New Fascists*, rev. ed. (London: Pan Books, 1983).
11. According to Carlos Marighela (fn. 3), "There is no longer any doubt that it is only through revolutionary action that an organization capable of carrying the revolution through to victory can be formed" (p. 30).

the sources of their beliefs. Most such organizations are concerned with justification and claim to act in the name of a set of principles.

A comparative analysis of the West German Red Army Fraction (RAF) and the Italian Red Brigades points to common elements in their philosophies, despite situational differences.[12] The author notes three significant characteristics of terrorist ideology in this type of organization: it is antagonistic to the beliefs of the majority of society; it reduces all political relationships to those of force and coercion, making compromise impossible; and the goals of its actions are indeterminate and vague.

The RAF claimed to represent a Marxist-Leninist intellectual heritage and its pronouncements were couched in the language of Marxist theory. However, since the German working class clearly rejected terrorism, the RAF dismissed the classical Marxist view of the objective conditions for revolution and focused instead on a subjective theory. Revolution was said to be possible if a committed and determined avant garde existed, regardless of the behavior of the masses. They borrowed elements of modern Marxism—the ideas of Lukacs, Marcuse and Habermas—to support their interpretation, but in general members of the Frankfurt School and the New Left were uncomfortable with this affiliation and distanced themselves from the terrorists.

In contrast, the Italian Red Brigades came from a political milieu in which violence was widely diffused but orthodox revolutionary Marxism had been abandoned. The perceived treachery of the Italian Communist Party (PCI) had embittered the far left. (The PCI took a firm anti-terrorist position, particularly after the 1978 kidnapping of Aldo Moro.) The Red Brigades attempted to distinguish themselves from other violent groups by adhering to a form of Marxism that the author of this analysis described as both archaic and Stalinist. Its central focus was the concept of an abstract "multinational imperialist state." The Red Brigades rejected the "spontaneity" and anarchism of rival terrorist groups such as Prima Linea.

Although beliefs may not motivate violence directly, ide-

---

12. This discussion is based on Francois Furet, Antoine Liniers and Philippe Raynaud, *Terrorisme et democratie* (Paris: Fayard, 1985), especially "Les origines intellectuelles du terrorism" by Philippe Raynaud.

ology appears to be functional to many individuals who embark on the course of terrorism. Their choice of ideology owes something to the surrounding political culture, but the original content of the ideas that terrorists start with may soon be lost or forgotten. Ideology becomes "surrealistic," used to escape a disconcerting reality rather than to guide actions. The extreme abstractness of such beliefs, especially with regard to the future, disconnects their holders from objective reality. This condition is likely to characterize the small revolutionary or right-wing underground that lacks social support. It means that as time passes terrorism becomes an end in itself, not a means of achieving political change.

The beliefs of extremists are not necessarily inflexible. Terrorists seem to modify their beliefs according to the context and political culture in which they operate. For example, in 1971 the Popular Front for the Liberation of Palestine changed its position on the usefulness of hijackings, a technique the group had initiated in 1968 and which had precipitated the 1970 Jordanian civil war. George Habash decreed that international operations were a manifestation of *petit bourgeois* spirit and adventurism. By 1987, Habash had declared extremism to be detrimental to the Palestinian national interest and condemned "strikes at imperialist interests" in the Middle East.[13]

The ideas that buttress the terrorism of right-wing extremists are even less systematic and logical than the beliefs of the far left. Fascism provides a convenient source for the doctrines of many European groups. Racism, anti-Communism and anti-Semitism are dominant motifs. However, the Italian group called the Third Position has adopted a confused theory of "Nazi-Maoism." The favorite reading material of young militants in Italy is apparently J.R.R. Tolkien's *The Lord of the Rings* trilogy. The American far right often shares the sentiments of racism and anti-Semitism, and sometimes espouses Christian fundamentalist beliefs.

The fact that terrorists are a tiny minority of those people exposed to any particular system of thought or political circumstances makes it difficult to accept ideology, religion, political culture or theories of relative deprivation as explanations for the sources of terrorism. Terrorism has no single cause. It is a

---

13. As'ad Abu Khalil, "Internal Contradictions in the PFLP: Decision Making and Policy Orientation," *Middle East Journal* 41 (1987), pp. 361–378.

product of psychological forces and group dynamics as much as the environment.

■ The Psychology of Terrorism

Researchers have begun to inquire carefully into the psychology of individuals who become terrorists, especially in Western liberal democracies where such behavior seems unjustified by circumstances.[14] Arguments based on the existence of a terrorist personality profile or psychopathological traits have largely been dismissed. Certainly the individuals who belong to Western terrorist organizations do not often present mental abnormalities, although it has been argued that the Italian far right exhibits more pathological traits than the left.[15] Nor are terrorists obviously characterized by any given set of psychological predispositions. The commitment to terrorism is what unites them.

The people who are stereotyped as "terrorists" actually perform a number of different roles within a dissident group, and their psychological requirements differ accordingly. These tasks can be highly specialized, especially in large and complex organizations. The person who makes a bomb, for example, or buys a gun, is unlikely to be the person who uses it. The leaders who make decisions do not implement them.

Conventional theories of behavior within political organizations could profitably be applied to terrorism. The incentives for participating in terrorism go beyond the fulfillment of an ideological commitment. Terrorists are not necessarily fanatical in their beliefs. In some situations the rewards for participation are social or financial. In others, involvement is a matter of political culture, not political choice. There is growing concern among psychologists that entire generations of potential ter-

---

14. See my review article, "The Psychology of Political Terrorism," in Margaret G. Hermann, ed., *Political Psychology* (San Francisco: Jossey-Bass, 1986). Two articles by Jeanne Knutson are especially interesting: "Social and Psychodynamic Pressures Toward a Negative Identity: The Case of an American Revolutionary Terrorist," in Yonah Alexander and John M. Gleason, eds., *Behavioral and Quantitative Perspectives on Terrorism* (New York: Pergamon, 1981); and "The Terrorists' Dilemmas: Some Implicit Rules of the Game," *Terrorism: An International Journal* 4 (1980), pp. 195–222.
15. Franco Ferracuti and Francesco Bruno, "Psychiatric Aspects of Terrorism in Italy," in K.L. Barak-Glantz and C. R. Huff, eds., *The Mad, The Bad and The Different* (Lexington, MA: D.C. Heath, 1981).

rorists are socialized into violence through the experience of living in an atmosphere of intensely violent conflict, such as in Belfast or Beirut. Terrorism becomes a natural response to frustration. This is not to say, however, that terrorism is always the product of circumstances, since only a few of the people who experience deprivation or violence react by turning to terrorism.

However, a body of information is slowly accumulating about individual terrorists. Most are young, certainly. This may account for their willingness to take risks and their ability to overcome the moral inhibitions that would prevent most people from using extreme violence in a way that defies social norms. It has also been suggested that terrorists are people whose identity formation is incomplete. Their immaturity makes them susceptible to extremist beliefs and to the power of the group and its leaders. Research has also indicated that the terrorist may be ambivalent about violence, uncomfortable with his or her own aggressive tendencies and likely to blame others rather than to accept responsibility for unpleasant outcomes. Rather than being amoral, they are likely to believe so strongly in the justice of their cause that they are able to distance themselves from their victims. Their self-righteousness is absolute. Most terrorists conceive of their actions as defensive and justified. They often imagine themselves as sacrificial victims or as avengers. Their self-conceptions are displayed in an elaborate military and legalistic terminology, a parody of the state. They are organized into columns, brigades and armies. In 1978 the Red Brigades held an elaborate "trial" of Aldo Moro, which resulted in his "execution." The Tupamaros of Uruguay held their kidnapped victims in "people's prisons."

Individual salvation may be as driving a motive as changing the world. Some undergrounds could be considered redemptive organizations, similar in many ways to religious cults. The apparent self-sacrifice or martyrdom seen recently in some bombings has reinforced the impression of terrorists who are willing and indeed eager to die for the cause. This image of the "suicide-bomber" is particularly frightening to the public because such intense devotion seems both irrational and unstoppable. However, such incidents are neither as ubiquitous nor as novel as much of the media coverage would have them be. Although rare, the phenomenon has been known since the nineteenth century. In any event, the term suicide is misleading as a psychological description of the mindset of such terrorists.

■ The Power of the Group

The group is more important than the individual to the dynamics of terrorism. Many people are recruited into terrorist organizations because of their need to belong to a community of like-minded individuals as much as to achieve political purposes. Students in West Germany, for example, belonged to communes or residential cooperatives and followed their friends and fellow residents into terrorism. The decision to resort to terrorism was not independent of the decision to remain in the group. Lebanese terrorism is also strongly associated with personal and family ties.

The group, furthermore, attains an immense power over the individual. The circumstances under which an extremist organization operates reinforce the tendencies toward cohesion and uniformity that are characteristic of all primary groups. The members face real danger, live in isolation from society, and are dependent for survival on each other and the group. Expression of dissent is stifled. From the point of view of the leadership, action may be essential to holding the group together. Terrorism may become self-sustaining, since action is required in order to maintain the group.

The psychological interdependence of members of such groups and their indoctrination into extreme loyalty toward the collectivity (necessary if dissent and factionalism are to be contained) may be reflected in the seizure of hostages in order to secure the release of imprisoned comrades. Terrorists may experience what is known as "survivor guilt," which makes them desperate to free their fellows. Their own fear of death or imprisonment can only be overcome by trying to save others. The demands for the freedom of prisoners in Kuwait, Cyprus or Israel may be genuine. They are not merely attempts to embarrass governments.

One also has to look at the universe in which radical groups operate. Most exist in a competitive environment. Their actions are responses to rivals as much as to government policies.[16] Despite pressures toward group conformity, faction-alism is rampant. The Palestinian resistance movement is an excellent example. Actions apparently directed against Israel or the United States may actually be meant to secure the ascen-dancy of a group over its rivals. The *Achille Lauro* affair in October 1985 could be seen as a move on the part of the Abu al-Abbas faction of the Palestinian Liberation Front (PLF) to block Arafat's Jordanian strategy. Any movement by Arafat toward compromise is met by the terrorism of the intransigent factions, particularly the Abu Nidal group, which opposes not only Arafat's goals but his personal leadership. It is well to remember that Palestinian moderates are frequently the targets of assassination attempts. Factionalism also makes it difficult to assign responsibility for specific terrorist actions.

■ The Effects of Terrorism

A last aspect of the diverse reality of terror-ism concerns its political and social consequences.

First, although much international terrorism is clearly anti-Western, it would be shortsighted to ignore its implica-tions for the East and for the Third World. The 1986 Karachi hijacking attempt was directed against an American airline en route to New York. However, the location of the attack was an Islamic country long sympathetic to Palestinian aspirations. The majority of victims were Indians whose prime minister was at that precise moment attending a meeting of nonaligned nations. Also in 1986, an Iraqi airliner was hijacked and crashed, killing 62 passengers. Islamic Jihad claimed responsi-bility. In 1985, four Soviet Embassy officials were among the foreigners kidnapped in Lebanon; one was killed, and the other three released. The hostages represent eighteen different nationalities. In 1985, 16 percent of the victims of international terrorism came from Arab League countries (in 1986, 10.9 percent). Citizens of Colombia, Iraq, Jordan, Libya and Nicara-gua, as well as Palestinians, all figured prominently as victims (although the United States headed the list with 17 percent, and 45 percent of victims and incidents were West European). In 1986, 4.4 percent of victims were from Warsaw Pact coun-

---

16. See Martha Crenshaw, "An Organizational Approach to the Analysis of Political Terrorism," *Orbis* 29 (1985), pp. 465-489.

tries (but over 50 percent from NATO countries). In 1987, 42 percent of terrorist victims were from NATO states, 16 percent from Arab League countries and none from the Warsaw Pact states. The United States suffered the most incidents with casualties (16 percent), but Pakistan was, a close second.

Second, despite this vulnerability to terrorism, the stability of Western political systems is not in jeopardy. Established liberal democracies have successfully withstood the challenges of internal and external terrorism. In fact, in many Western states terrorism has resulted in more powerful coercive institutions and capabilities. Public support for vigorous anti-terrorist measures has grown. Israeli policy analyst Yehezkel Dror has argued effectively that liberal democracies remain quite "robust" and that the challenge of terrorism may strengthen democratic governments.[17] If terrorism is meant to bring about radical political change, it has failed.

Third World regimes are more likely to experience major political change connected with terrorism, although it is difficult to make causal attributions. Regimes fell after revolutionary campaigns involving terrorism in five instances in the past twenty years: Nicaragua, Iran, Uruguay, Argentina and Turkey. In the first two cases, terrorism was an auxiliary strategy to a mass-based insurrection. In Nicaragua, where terrorism was extremely minor, the revolutionary organization remains in power. In Iran, the secular revolutionary forces soon parted ways with the regime of the Ayatollah Khomeini and turned in futility to terrorism against religious rule. In Uruguay, the inability of the government to control Tupamaro terrorism was one part of a complicated political and economic situation that led to a military overthrow of the civilian regime. In Argentina, the terrorism of the Montoneros and the ERP (Ejercito Revolucionario del Pueblo) also proved to be the final straw for the weak civilian regime of Peron's widow Isabel. The result again was a military dictatorship (and thousands of "disappearances" in the ensuing repression). In Turkey, uncontrollable terrorism of the right and of the left provoked a *coup d'etat* by the military in 1980. During the 1980s, India and Sri Lanka

---

17. "Terrorism as a Challenge to the Democratic Capacity to Govern," in Martha Crenshaw, ed., *Terrorism, Legitimacy and Power* (Middletown, CT: Wesleyan University Press, 1983).

experienced high levels of domestic political violence that strained democratic values.

In an earlier period, terrorism was associated with anti-colonialism. The Irgun zvai Leumi in Mandate Palestine and the FLN in Algeria are often cited as successful users of terrorism, but it is impossible to be precise about the role played by terrorism in bringing about independence in these contexts. Certainly nationalist terrorism and, perhaps more important, the military reaction to terrorism contributed to the growth of negative public opinion in Britain and France, sentiments that encouraged the British and French governments to withdraw from their respective Mediterranean possessions. It would be misleading, however, to associate the success of revolutionary or independence movements with terrorism. The reasons for revolutionary victories lie elsewhere.

The consequences of terrorism for international order are as yet obscure. They include general perceptions of loss of state control over the international environment, widening insecurities and deepening ideological divisions. Uncertainty is heightened, to the detriment of international cooperation. The everyday life of diplomats and travellers is disrupted. Among nations one sees mounting distrust and trading of charges and countercharges of complicity or negligence. The most visible effects of terrorism lie in the reactions of governments, which include rigorous security measures, diplomatic sanctions and the occasional resort to military force. The use of military force, a unilateral response to terrorism, includes rescues of hostages, apprehension of suspected terrorists, and retaliation, which is potentially the most damaging form of response for international order. In July 1976, Israel intervened successfully in Uganda to rescue hijacked airline passengers, and in October 1977, West Germany deployed a specialized military unit to free a Lufthansa jet in Mogadishu, Somalia. By the 1980s all Western states had created elite military intervention units for hostage rescues. The Israeli and West German units appeared encouraging as models for resolving the dilemma of hostage seizures, which otherwise left governments with no recourse but to make a deal or see their citizens killed. The United States, however, failed tragically to secure the release of kidnapped Embassy employees in Iran in 1980.

Israel has systematically resorted to both overt and covert

force in retaliation against Palestinian targets and in attempts to seize or kill suspected terrorists. Under the Reagan Administration, U.S. policy was based on the assumption that the doctrines of preemption and deterrence are applicable to terrorism. In 1985, an Egyptian aircraft carrying the presumed hijackers of the *Achille Lauro* was intercepted by American military jets and forced to land at an American base in Sicily. In 1986, U.S. forces conducted bombing raids against Libya as a retaliatory measure. For the United States, attempts to apprehend terrorists abroad are likely to become more frequent since legislation was passed in 1984 and 1986 that extended American extraterritorial criminal jurisdiction.

Other disturbing aspects of terrorism include unintended consequences. For example, terrorism can serve as a pretext for military intervention. The 1982 Israeli invasion of Lebanon was justified as a reply to the attempted assassination of the Israeli ambassador to London. Terrorism can force a government's hand. Public revelations of the Syrian ambassador's involvement in an attempted bombing of an El Al airliner in 1986 precipitated a rupture of diplomatic relations between the United Kingdom and Syria that was not regarded as desirable by either side.

The power of terrorism lies in its negative effects, which are most clearly in evidence in the contemporary Middle East. International terrorism is not a constructive political force, even if it does attract the attention of outside actors and sometimes alter their foreign policy commitments. Although the resort to terrorism in the early 1970s may have helped the PLO to gain international recognition, after 1975 mainstream PLO elements realized that it was incompatible with a search for political respectability or the status of *interlocuteur valable*. In 1988, Arafat's explicit renunciation of terrorism and American acceptance of that rejection were promising signs, but it is imperative that terrorism not be allowed to continue to place moderates at the mercy of extremists. Terrorism has contributed significantly to the intensification of conflict in the Middle East. It obstructs resolution of the problem of Palestine and heightens disorder in Lebanon. Ending terrorism and resolving political conflict are mutually interdependent objectives.

3

Possibilities for International Cooperation

■ The Current Status of Cooperation

Although the international community appears to recognize the need for cooperation against terrorism, national interests have dominated the treatment of the issue and unanimity has been rhetorical rather than practical. The situation remains, according to a French analyst, "chaotic."[18] At the global level, collaborative measures are formal and redundant, adopted as a reaction to events. There can be no doubt that sensitivity to the political implications of the issue of terrorism has limited international cooperation. The search for juridical solutions in the United Nations has not been notably successful.

Without tracing the history of attempts to bring concerted international effort to bear on the problem, it should be noted that in 1937 the League of Nations agreed to a Convention for the Suppression of Terrorism and establishment of a world criminal court. The issue of oppositional terrorism appeared on the international agenda of the post-World-War-II world only in 1972, as a result of the attack by the Black September organization on Israeli athletes at the Munich Olympic Games. An American initiative (the Draft Convention for the Prevention and Punishment of Certain Acts of International Terrorism) was rejected. Subsequent efforts to draw up treaties to submit to the General Assembly foundered on the issue of defining terrorism, which split Third World and Western states. Their differences centered on the issue of whether

---

18. Stéphane Vérine, "La coopération internationale en matière de lutte contre le terrorisme," *Politique Etrangère* 4 (1986), p. 977.

terrorism can be considered in isolation from its causes, which the Third World conceived to be racism and colonialism. The Third World insisted that state "terrorism" or oppression was the real priority.

However, as oppositional terrorism came to threaten more and more states, a body of international law developed in specific and limited areas. Its approach was not to make "terrorism" a crime, given the imprecision and ambiguity of the term, but to outlaw the specific actions that are the components of terrorist strategies, such as hijackings or attacks on diplomatic agents. In 1973, the Convention on Prevention and Punishment of Crimes Against Internationally Protected Persons, Including Diplomatic Agents urged international coordination to prevent attacks on diplomats. In 1979, the General Assembly adopted the International Convention Against the Taking of Hostages. Finally, in December 1985, the General Assembly passed a resolution condemning terrorism regardless of occasion or cause. The resolution also called on member nations to sign the relevant multilateral treaties, which include three anti-hijacking agreements negotiated under the auspices of the International Civil Aviation Organization, the 1969 Tokyo Convention (the Convention on Offenses and Certain Other Acts Committed on Board Aircraft), the 1970 Hague Convention (the Convention for the Suppression of Unlawful Seizure of Aircraft) and the 1971 Montreal Convention (the Convention for the Suppression of Unlawful Acts Against Safety of Civil Aviation). In general, these multilateral treaties require states to extradite any alleged offenders apprehended on their territory or to submit their cases to the appropriate local authorities for prosecution.

Implementation of the conventions has been inconsistent, however. John F. Murphy, expressing a general consensus among American international law specialists, concludes: "The effectiveness of these global conventions as antiterrorist measures is questionable. Even if fully implemented, the limited and piecemeal solutions of these conventions would be of little use in combatting the many manifestations of terrorism."[19] British scholar Paul Wilkinson is more pointed: "The United

---

19. John F. Murphy, "The Future of Multilateralism and Efforts to Combat International Terrorism," *Columbia Journal of Transnational Law* 35 (1986), p. 44.

Nations has proved a broken reed on the whole subject of terrorism. It has proved as useless in countering terrorism as the League of Nations before it."[20] He attributes failure even within Western Europe to lack of political will and the jealous regard for national sovereignties rather than technical and legal complexities. Abraham D. Sofaer, Legal Adviser to the U.S. Department of State, argues that international law is not only unhelpful but "perverse" in its demonstration of lack of agreement.[21] He cites the United Nations debates over the 1985 resolution, certainly the high point of United Nations cooperation, as evidence of a severe lack of consensus rather than progress toward international unity.

Many Western observers agree that realistically the United Nations is not the best forum for cooperation against terrorism. In fact, in the U.S. perspective, inability to agree on condemning terrorism has discredited the United Nations. In general, the larger the number of actors involved, the more difficult it is to achieve cooperation in any area. Given the universal scope of UN treaties, as well as the controversial nature of terrorism, it is not surprising that international treaties are often ineffective because of undersubscription and reluctant implementation. The perceived inadequacy of the United Nations has caused Western states to seek the establishment of separate models for cooperation at regional levels.

The Organization of American States was the first regional international organization to react to terrorism, particularly diplomatic kidnappings, with the 1971 Convention to Prevent and Punish the Acts of Terrorism Taking the Form of Crimes Against Persons and Related Extortion That are of International Significance, largely superseded by the 1973 UN Convention on Protected Persons. In 1977 the Council of Europe drew up the European Convention on the Suppression of Terrorism, which attempted to restrict the use of the political offense exception to extradition, probably the most formidable legal barrier to cooperation. The European Communities reached an agreement in Dublin to apply the convention to member-states in 1979. However, not even all West European states have signed the treaty. France is not yet a party to either

---

20. Paul Wilkinson, *Terrorism and the Liberal State*, rev. ed. (New York: New York University Press, 1986), p. 284.
21. "Terrorism and the Law," *Foreign Affairs* 64 (1986), pp. 901-922.

the European Convention or the Dublin Agreement. Murphy describes the state of these measures as "relative impotence."[22]

The diplomatic coordination among Western states that has occurred at the seven-power economic summits has become much more meaningful as a symbol of cooperation than international treaties, even though the summit statements are not binding in international law. According to Robert D. Putnam and Nicholas Bayne, no other international body matches the effectiveness of the summits for expressing Western interests.[23] Since 1978, terrorism has been regularly considered at the summits, which are designed to be flexible and unstructured. Originally they were meant to be exchanges of personal views among leaders. The joint statements issued by the summits have become increasingly specific about measures to be undertaken and increasingly expansive in scope. Terrorism and international public order were one of the two major themes of political discussions at the summits, second only to East-West relations and arms control. In 1986, the Tokyo declaration on terrorism was the main achievement of the heads of government in the political arena.

In the 1980s, terrorism was repeatedly discussed at high levels in other Western institutions. In early 1986, the European Community established a Committee of Foreign Ministers to deal with the issue. The subject frequently appears on the agenda of the Council of Europe and the European Parliament. The North Atlantic Assembly (the association of parliamentarians of the NATO countries) established a Working Group on Terrorism, which issued a formal report in 1987. The United States, however, was not successful in establishing a NATO standing committee.

Networks of informal cooperation also exist at lower levels of government. In 1976, the European Community established the "Trevi" system of working groups linking Ministries of Justice and the Interior. The measures agreed upon at meetings of the Trevi group, to which the United States is invited, include sharing information, improving communications among European police forces, coordinating visa arrangements

---

22. John F. Murphy, "The Future of Multilateralism," p. 62.
23. Robert D. Putnam and Nicholas Bayne, *Hanging Together: Cooperation and Conflict in the Seven-Power Summits* (Cambridge: Harvard University Press, 1987), pp. 222, 241.

and reviewing extradition procedures, airport security and abuses of diplomatic immunity.

In 1984, the General Assembly of the International Criminal Police Organization (Interpol), which has 136 members, removed restrictions on sharing information on terrorism. The Interpol Constitution prohibits member countries from intervention in or investigations of military, political, religious or racial matters, but the Interpol General Assembly resolved that violence committed outside the area of conflict or against innocent victims should not be considered as political in this sense. Ironically, debate over this issue began in 1950 when Czechoslovakian refugees hijacked an airplane and sought asylum abroad. The United States withdrew from active participation in protest against Interpol's acquiescence to a request from Czechoslovakia (then a member) to issue arrest notices.[24]

There is also a substantial area of bilateral cooperation in dealing with terrorism. In the areas of extradition and aviation security the United States has bilateral treaties in force with 29 nations.[25] In general, the Reagan Administration tried to restrict the use of the political offense exception in new and revised extradition treaties, such as the Supplementary Extradition Treaty with the United Kingdom (1986). U.S. bilateral treaties include a 1986 agreement on aviation security with the Soviet Union. The United States also has an aviation security treaty with Yugoslavia. In 1973, in the wake of a series of hijackings from the United States to Cuba, the United States signed a Memorandum of Understanding with Cuba, providing for the return of hijacked aircraft and the extradition or prosecution of hijackers. This document is often thought of as a model for agreements between politically opposed governments that nevertheless find particular actions mutually objectionable. Ad hoc bilateral cooperation between East and West can also be significant, as when Hungary assisted with the Vienna airport bombing in December 1985. The U.S. State Department also maintains an anti-terrorism assistance program, which provides training and law enforcement assistance.

---

24. See *TVI Journal* 6 (1985), pp. 3–12.
25. The texts of bilateral and multilateral agreements, summit statements, and U.S. laws can be found in *International Terrorism: A Compilation of Major Laws, Treaties, Agreements, and Executive Documents,* a report prepared for the Committee on Foreign Affairs of the U.S. House of Representatives by the Congressional Research Service (1987).

Between 1983 and 1987, forty-three Third World and Western countries participated in its activities.

The United States has tended to bypass the United Nations and to seek agreement only among "like-minded" states.[26] As John F. Murphy argues, the Reagan Administration was not a strong supporter of multilateralism in the conduct of U.S. foreign policy.[27] The administration was generally suspicious of "world government" types of institutions, and the UN and its specialized agencies had minimal impact on the formulation of U.S. foreign policy. The prospects for East-West cooperation took second place to transatlantic cooperation in this area. However, if American policymakers genuinely believe that the Soviet Union and the Eastern bloc provide essential aid to terrorist groups, then the task of convincing them to join in collective measures takes on special importance.

■ Changing Soviet Attitudes

Another reason for a fresh look at the possibilities of strengthened international cooperation against terrorism is that, since Gorbachev's accession to power, the Soviet Union has expressed a new and specific interest in reducing international terrorism. In his speech to the 27th Congress of the CPSU in 1987, Gorbachev proposed that the development of effective ways of combating international terrorism be made part of a comprehensive international security system. Professor Aleksander Kislov of the Institute of World Economics and International Relations in Moscow argues that terrorism "has nowadays become one of the most acute international problems, constituting a serious threat to the cause of peace, security, and international cooperation." He adds that "the Soviet Union rejects terrorism on principle and is ready to cooperate thoroughly with other states in its eradication."[28]

The Soviet Union now appears to recognize that national security is related to the mutual interdependence of nations

---

26. Parker W. Borg, "International Terrorism: Breaking the Cycle of Violence," Occasional Paper No. 8, Foreign Service Institute (Washington, DC: U.S. Department of State, 1987).

27. See, for example, John F. Murphy, "The Future of Multilateralism."

28. Aleksander Kislov, "Prospects for Cooperation between East and West in Dealing with Terrorism," paper presented to the conference on International Aspects of Terrorism, Netherlands Institute of International Relations, June 1987.

and the necessity for restraint: "Respect for the norms of international law becomes a matter of mankind's survival today because the security of each state depends on the security of other states and the whole of mankind, and not on the quantity and even quality of their own weapons and armed forces." Furthermore, "All states today face a fundamental task: without closing their eyes to the social, political and ideological differences they must learn to act with restraint and circumspection on the international scene, to live in a civilized way, and to behave correctly in international communication and cooperation."[29]

These changes seem to be more than rhetorical. Soviet policy toward the Third World and national liberation movements appears to be undergoing parallel revisions, although the meaning of these changes in thinking and behavior is a source of dispute among Western analysts. While acknowledging this division of opinion, Neil MacFarlane argues that under Gorbachev's leadership Soviet attitudes and policy are entering a new phase.[30] Official comment on the Third World in general has become rare, and even less notice is given to revolutionary movements. Expressions of willingness to provide military assistance for revolutionary movements are few; in general revolutionaries are advised to help themselves. Revolutionary conflicts are explicitly delinked from the global configuration of power. The Soviet Union appears sensitive to the potentially damaging consequences for relations with the United States if competition in the Third World is conducted at acute levels. The Soviet Union appears less willing to allow clashes over these issues to jeopardize progress in areas such as arms control. In addition, the Soviet Union is more inclined to stress the local sources of conflict, including non-class factors such as religion, ethnicity and nationalism. MacFarlane concludes: "The impression one gets here is that Soviet experts have come to see the Third World as far more complex and dangerous terrain than they had previously thought."[31] Gorbachev has been particularly solicitous of India, a country plagued by

---

29. Igor Lukashuk and Rein Mullerson, "State Terrorism and International Law," *International Affairs* (February 1987), p. 80.
30. Neil MacFarlane, "The USSR and The Third World: Continuity and Change under Gorbachev," *The Harriman Institute Forum* 1, No. 3 (March 1988), pp. 1–7.
31. Ibid., p. 3.

separatist terrorism that includes attacks on civil aviation targets abroad (and formerly revolutionary terrorism practiced by the Naxalite movement, or the Communist Party of India-Marxist-Leninist). In the Middle East, the Soviet Union has expressed interest in a nonmilitary solution to the Arab-Israeli conflict as well as in the restoration of diplomatic relations with Israel. Israel's prompt return of a hijacked Soviet airliner in the fall of 1988 symbolized the improving relationship. Moscow has also supported United Nations peacekeeping operations.

The Israeli analyst Galia Golan agrees that since Gorbachev there has been "an almost total absence of references to national liberation movements."[32] The Soviet Union shows little interest in commitments to national liberation struggles, possibly because of the risks such involvements create for other policies, the lack of concrete returns on these investments of scarce resources and the lessons of Afghanistan. In general, the Soviet Union is anti-separatist, but it supports the PLO as "anticolonial." On the same grounds, the Soviet Union has aided the African National Congress. But the PLO is dissatisfied with the level of assistance provided by the Soviet Union, whose aid has been sporadic and whose behavior has been cautious. Moscow prefers Arafat and Fatah to the smaller groups that have been the more avid practitioners of international terrorism (which Arafat disavows), particularly the Popular Front for the Liberation of Palestine and the Democratic Front for the Liberation of Palestine. Apparently Moscow has questioned the effectiveness of the Palestinian use of terrorism, but has not so far made its support contingent upon the approval of specific methods: "Moscow has not been heavily influenced by the methodology of a movement, although it has expressed preferences for conventional warfare over guerrilla warfare, sabotage over terror, and political struggle over armed struggle."[33] At the same time, the Soviet Union definitely wants to prevent American intervention in the Middle East. Since terrorism is likely to increase rather than decrease American involvement, the pragmatic course is to discourage terrorism.

---

32. Galia Golan, "Moscow and Third World National Liberation Movements: The Soviet Role," *Journal of International Affairs* 40 (1987), p. 306.
33. Ibid., p. 315.

Recent Soviet reactions to specific incidents of anti-Western terrorism also signal stronger condemnation of such tactics, although the Soviet Union continues to blame U.S. policy for terrorism and to name state terrorism as the greater problem. In 1985 the Soviet Union called U.S. anger over the *Achille Lauro* hijacking and the murder of passenger Leon Klinghoffer "understandable and just," and called for severe punishment of the terrorists, who were members of the Palestine Liberation Front (PLF).[34] In response to the September 1986 hijacking attempt by the Abu Nidal faction (Fatah Revolutionary Council) against a U.S. airliner in Pakistan which resulted in twenty-one deaths, a commentator in *Pravda* issued a sharply critical statement: "No matter what the motives of the people who committed this evil deed, there is no justifying it . . . . A resolute stop must be put to terrorism of all sorts . . . . These criminal actions must not be allowed to end people's lives, jeopardize the normal course of international relations, severely exacerbate some situation or other, or engender violence. . . ."[35] The rash of bombings in Paris in the fall of 1986 was condemned with equal severity.

Furthermore, the Soviet reaction to American military retaliation against Libya in 1986 for its complicity in international terrorist activity was muted. Although the Soviet Union protested by cancelling a summit planning meeting between Foreign Minister Eduard A. Shevardnadze and Secretary of State George P. Shultz, still Moscow failed to warn Libya of the impending raid despite the fact that "implicitly the prospect of American retaliatory action had been discussed in advance with the Soviets."[36] Gorbachev appeared unwilling to allow the raid to impede the normalization of relations with the United States, especially since Soviet relations with Libya were already strained, as indicated by the earlier Soviet refusal to sign a treaty of friendship and cooperation. As one analyst noted, "Quaddafi can find little solace in the Soviet response. While

---

34. *The Washington Post*, October 12, 1985, p. 21, quoting *TASS*.
35. P. Demchenko, "There is No Justification for Terrorism," *Pravda*, September 9, 1986, in *Current Digest of the Soviet Press* 38 (October 8, 1986), p. 17.
36. *The Christian Science Monitor*, April 23, 1986, p. 13. See also *The Washington Post*, April 19, 1986, p. 21. European sources indicated that the Soviet Union initiated a hot-line conversation with the United States (*Europe*, April 14–15 and 16, 1986; quoted in Juliet Lodge, ed., *The Threat of Terrorism* [Boulder, CO: Westview Press, 1988], p. 245).

denouncing the attack, the Soviet government was careful to maintain a certain distance from Quaddafi, apparently unwilling to risk a conflict with the United States over what has proved to be a most unpredictable partner."[37] In January 1989 the Soviet Union was similarly circumspect when U.S. Navy fighters shot down two Libyan MIGs over the Mediterranean. Although the U.S. action was officially labeled "state terrorism," the Soviet Union did not heed Libyan requests for military assistance.

Nor did the Soviet Union react to charges that its longtime ally Syria was involved in anti-Western terrorism. These accusations, offered by the Italian, West German, Spanish and U.K. governments, culminated in October 1986 in the U.K. government's severing of diplomatic relations with Syria in light of a U.K. court verdict implicating Syrian officials in the attempted bombing of an El Al airliner in London (a link that Assad denied).[38] In the United Nations in December 1987 the Soviet Union and many Third World nations joined the West in the General Assembly to defeat a Syrian proposal that many countries considered a highly provocative attempt to legitimize international terrorism.[39] Syria had called on the United Nations to convene an international conference to define the difference between terrorism and the legitimate right of oppressed peoples to fight for national freedom. Soviet opposition to the proposed conference was apparently the "last straw" isolating Syria. The result was a compromise resolution that reaffirmed the earlier United Nations stand against international terrorism.

The Soviet Union has frequently reiterated its interest in strengthening international cooperation. After the Karachi hijacking, Tass was authorized to express resolute condemnation and rejection of terrorism as well as an appeal to "all states to engage in effective cooperation to wipe out this dangerous phenomenon."[40] In late 1986 and early 1987 reports in the American press suggested that the Soviet Union was increasingly concerned over being identified with groups using

---

37. Ronald Bruce St. John, "Terrorism and Libyan Foreign Policy, 1981–1986," *The World Today* 42 (1986), p. 114.
38. See Moshe Ma'oz, "State-Run Terrorism in the Middle East: The Case of Syria," *Middle East Review* 1, No. 3 (Spring, 1987), pp. 11–15.
39. *The New York Times*, December 2, 1987, p. A17.
40. Reported in *Current Digest of the Soviet Press* 38 (October 8, 1986), p. 17.

terrorism. It is reasonable to suspect that public exposure of Libyan and Syrian connections to attacks on civilian targets was embarrassing. Western diplomats were said to believe that the free movement of members of such groups across East European borders was being curtailed and that some Arab diplomats were being placed under surveillance.[41] Hungary was said to have passed information to Western governments with regard to the Rome and Vienna airport attacks in December 1985, and to have agreed to work with the United States against terrorism. There was speculation that the incidence of terrorism in Western Europe has decreased because of restrictions on "safe havens" in the East.[42] It was further reported that "the Soviet Union has asked several Western governments to cooperate with it in fighting international terrorism and has suggested that they negotiate extradition treaties providing for the return of terrorist suspects. . . . Diplomats say this is the first time the Soviet Union has begun what appears to be a concerned diplomatic campaign to convince Western governments that it disapproves of terrorism and is ready to cooperate with them in combatting it."[43] Further evidence of an Eastern interest in cooperation is seen in the offer made by Czechoslovakia to assist in investigating the explosives used in the December 1988 Pan Am bombing.

The agreement on human rights reached by the Conference on Security and Cooperation in Europe in January 1989 is additional proof of Soviet and East European interest in cooperating with the West against terrorism. The agreement, signed by the United States, Canada, the Soviet Union and all European nations except Albania, contains a provision condemning terrorism as unjustifiable under any circumstances. It calls for firmness in response to demands, strengthened international cooperation, tighter national controls over groups that perpetrate acts of terrorism and extradition or prosecution of persons responsible for terrorism. Although not legally binding, the document is regarded as a significant guarantee of human rights (see Appendix, Document 4).

41. *The New York Times*, December 19, 1986, p. 15.
42. *The Christian Science Monitor*, March 20, 1987, p. 1.
43. *The New York Times*, April 1, 1987, p. 3.

4

Conditions for Future Cooperation

If the evidence is persuasive that a common interest exists between East and West in dealing with terrorism, what are the conditions for cooperation? This analysis is based on the assumption that cooperation is necessary precisely because political differences exist. The purpose of cooperation is not to create a harmony of interests but to agree on a minimum level of behavior each nation expects from others. Cooperation means that a nation must occasionally be willing to alter its policies in order to benefit others. This analysis also assumes that agreement among states on a subject usually precedes the development of international law in the area. International law does not create international order. Nor does cooperation have to be institutionalized, although institutions facilitate cooperative behavior.

The lessons of the Western summits are instructive because they can be applied to East-West cooperation. According to Putnam and Bayne, the issue of terrorism was suitable for agreement for several reasons.[44] It was less technically complex than arms control. There was no awkward overlap with NATO responsibilities. The issue involved a complicated mixture of domestic and foreign factors, which meant that there was an important role for heads of government in reconciling divergent needs. Domestic public opinion wanted decisive action, which compelled the attention of top political leaders. Dealing with such a complex issue required the coordination of many different national bureaucracies.

The 1986 Tokyo summit succeeded in restoring allied unity, undermined by the U.S. raid on Libya. In practical terms,

---

44. Putnam and Bayne, *Hanging Together*, p. 244.

the summit created a network of official groups on terrorism. However, foreign policy analysis and treatment of the causes of terrorism were neglected because of the U.S. preoccupation with condemning Libya. Domestic and international pressures were conflicting, since the United States wanted international endorsement of actions already decided on for domestic reasons rather than a negotiated compromise. The revelation that the United States was pursuing secret arms deals with Iran while insisting on sanctions and retaliation against Libya later made the summit agreement appear hypocritical. The Europeans were more honest in their approach and moved significantly toward greater cooperation.[45]

The summit experience is a reminder that nations frequently enter into cooperative arrangements in order to placate domestic constituencies rather than to reach working agreements. It is also a reminder that agreements are often precipitated by crisis. Cooperation is not necessarily based on common understanding of issues. In such cases, it may be superficial and short-lived.

Other requirements of cooperation can be analyzed by borrowing from realist theories of international politics and from game theory. The conditions for cooperation can be summarized in the following abstract terms:[46]

1. The rules of cooperative behavior must be defined.
2. The mutual benefits of cooperation must be clear.
3. The distinction between cooperation and non-cooperation must be apparent.
4. The penalties for not cooperating must be recognized.

■ Rule-making

One of the problems in establishing international cooperation on the issue of terrorism is that common rules for behavior have yet to be established. In other areas, such as the conduct of warfare, economic relationships or arms control, rules exist. Traditions are sanctioned by long experience. With regard to terrorism, a common set of norms and expectations is lacking. Terrorism is still a relatively new issue

---

45. Ibid., pp. 244–246.
46. See Putnam and Bayne, *Hanging Together;* and Kenneth Oye, ed., Special Issue of *World Politics* 38 (1985), pp. 1–254. See also Robert Jervis, "Cooperation under the Security Dilemma," *World Politics* 30 (January 1978), pp. 157–180.

for international politics. There is little consensus on what the problem is, much less on what measures would offer an effective solution.

The world of international relations is often thought of as a game, or as a multilayered combination of different and overlapping games. One of the centerpieces of realist theories of international politics is the "stag hunt" analogy of Jean-Jacques Rousseau, alluded to by Kenneth Waltz in his classic book, *Man, the State, and War*.[47] He compares the world of nations to a group of hunters banded together to catch a stag. If all remain in their places in the circle, they will catch the stag and each will obtain a generous supply of meat. However, what happens if a rabbit runs past? The hunter who abandons the circle in order to catch the rabbit will certainly have something to eat—less than his share of the stag, but sufficient for his short-term needs. The others, however, will have nothing because the cooperation of all is required in order to catch the stag. Each hunter must reasonably fear that one of his neighbors will desert the circle. The individual who fears the consequences of the defection of others may opt for the certain if lesser gain of the rabbit. Uncertainty about the intentions of others encourages uncooperative and ultimately self-defeating behavior.

In the metaphorical game of the stag hunt, as in many areas of international relations, the meaning of cooperation is clear to all parties. In the international game nations are forced into cooperation by terrorism; however, the specific requirements of cooperation remain to be negotiated.

It can easily be seen that many of the rules that some states wish to see implemented are in themselves highly controversial, such as the recommendation that extradition be made automatic. Restricting the political offense exception has proved extraordinarily difficult even among the liberal democracies of the European communities. The statements resulting from Western summit meetings contain the following substantive (not procedural) recommendations of what the rules ought to be:
- cessation of flights to countries that refuse to extradite or prosecute hijackers, and curtailment of the rights of their national airlines;

---

47. (New York: Columbia University Press, 1959).

- consultations and exchanges of information in cases of terrorism against diplomats;

- an international response to states shown to be assisting terrorist groups, including prohibiting the sale of weapons to such states and restricting the size of their diplomatic missions;

- revisions of national legislation, in order to implement anti-terrorist policies and bring national laws into accord with treaty obligations;

- denial of entry, expulsion or exclusion of known terrorists, and tightened immigration and visa regulations;

- improved extradition procedures;

- closer coordination of domestic bureaucracies, including intelligence exchanges; and

- no concessions to terrorist demands in hostage seizures.

The United States favors measures that would demonstrate an international consensus against terrorism. In addition, Parker W. Borg, formerly with the U.S. Department of State's Office of the Ambassador at Large for Counter-Terrorism, has suggested several other specific U.S. policy interests worth considering: an appropriate forum for discussions on terrorism, extending beyond the "Summit Seven"; and better information-sharing, not of sensitive government intelligence but general knowledge about terrorism, perhaps involving the adoption of a common reporting format after incidents. He also recommends discussion of covert operations and the appropriate deployment and structuring of military counter-terrorist forces.[48]

Several sources, most unofficial, have also recommended that a joint Western military intervention team be created. This suggestion is found, for example, in the 1987 report from the North Atlantic Assembly. Such a multinational force would assist in hostage rescues and would compensate for the lack of intervention capabilities in smaller states which otherwise might be reluctant to invite foreign forces to undertake rescue missions. Furthermore, having a European team would make it unnecessary for the United States to ask its allies to permit the prepositioning of American special operations forces during hostages crises.

---

48. See Parker W. Borg, "International Terrorism" (fn. 26).

In 1988, the United Kingdom urged greater cooperation in protecting civil aviation. One recommendation was that the International Civil Aviation Organization (ICAO) establish an experts' group to advise governments during hijackings. Another was that airport security guidelines be made mandatory. These recommendations have received special attention since the December 1988 Pan Am bombing.

Professor Kislov's paper on the prospects of cooperation mentions other steps, which one assumes the Soviet government finds acceptable:[49]

- an international conference under UN auspices to define terrorism and work toward a universal convention;
- energetic national measures, such as, for example, to provide punishment for acts of international terrorism, enact stricter prohibitions on sales and possession of weapons and on training camps, and work toward more responsible media coverage of terrorism;
- greater involvement of states in existing international agreements;
- definition and specification of the rights and duties of states involved as victims, patrons or unwilling hosts for terrorism;
- exchanges of information, in the context of regional or bilateral agreements; and
- study of the possibility for establishing a permanent agency in the UN to specialize in preventing terrorism.

In 1987, the Soviet delegation to the Conference on Security and Cooperation in Europe proposed convening an expert conference on preventing international terrorism.

An agenda for discussion could be constructed out of these proposals. For example, points of agreement include persuading all states to approve existing cooperative arrangements and to implement more energetic domestic measures. It is worth noting that some measures that are controversial among Western countries would not be in an East-West context, such as "no concessions." At the same time, several proposals from the Eastern bloc might be unacceptable to the West, such as general United Nations conferences or committees, due to their poor track record, although the United States favors UN resolutions condemning attacks on civil aviation or abuses of diplomatic

---

49. See Aleksander Kislov, "Prospects for Cooperation" (fn. 28).

privileges and immunities. Nor are restrictions on media coverage likely to be attractive options, despite the United Kingdom's recent restrictions on coverage of IRA violence. It is unrealistic to expect routine East-West intelligence or technology exchanges. Nevertheless, there appears to be some common ground to be explored.

■ Rewards for Cooperation

Assuming that mutually agreeable rules for cooperation in combatting terrorism can be found, how can cooperation be made rewarding? Furthermore, can it be established that the assistance of all states is required for effective cooperation and the consequent acquisition of a mutual good? Can the opposite be shown, that defection or noncooperation is harmful to all members of the international community?

The first question is whether the forms of cooperation suggested by various parties would end terrorism. For example, if the U.S. recommendation that no state ever meet terrorists' demands were universally obeyed, would terrorism decline? In 1981 the RAND Corporation suggested that the evidence that such a policy works was "meager and unconvincing."[50] Some analysts, however, contend that a consistent no-concessions policy has never been implemented, which leaves no way of evaluating its effectiveness. Nevertheless, it is impossible to know whether the United States would have suffered more terrorist attacks if American willingness to concede had been greater. The issue that is relevant for international cooperation is whether a collective no-concessions posture is more effective than a national policy. Although the 1986 Tokyo summit declaration included such a prohibition, it has not been uniformly observed. Logic would lead one to expect that in a world in which some states resist demands and others acquiesce, terrorism would be drawn to those who yield. However, terrorist motives are not always perfectly logical. Terrorism against the United States is attractive regardless of the American stance on concessions. But international cooperation would be easier if it could be demonstrated that a unilateral effort by a state to increase its security by making deals with terrorists

---

50. Gail Bass, Brian M. Jenkins, Konrad Kellen and David Ronfeldt, *Options for U.S. Policy on Terrorism* (Santa Monica: RAND, 1981), p. 5.

necessarily decreases the security of others. This problem reflects what realist theories of international politics term the "security dilemma."

In general, the effects of policies toward terrorism are hard to demonstrate. Very little is known about how terrorism declines. Terrorists may respond to internal dynamics as much as to government policy. A combination of internal and external pressures that undermine group cohesion and morale and provoke organizational disintegration is probably critical. Decreased support from constituencies, perception of the failure of terrorism as a means and the loss of sanctuaries or staging areas combine to bring about the decline of international terrorism. Most groups that use terrorism have constituencies whose approval they seek. If it becomes clear that a group's own national or ethnic community rejects its methods, it may reevaluate the strategy. Failure can lead to demoralization, as it did among West European groups. In many cases, the direct responses of the targets of terrorism may matter less to terrorists than changes in the attitudes of supporters. The self-conceptions of the terrorists themselves are more likely to be affected by the attitudes of friends than by those of enemies. Competition among groups and doctrinal disagreements may be aggravated by external events. This process may be initiated by an egregiously indiscriminate or unjustifiable terrorist act that generates dissent and disillusionment. The 1983 Orly bombing, for example, apparently disillusioned many Armenians who consequently withdrew their support for the Armenian Secret Army for the Liberation of Armenia (ASALA). In miscalculating the effects of their actions, terrorists may bring about their own downfall.

Nevertheless, in examining shifts in terrorist behavior it is apparent that the loss of foreign bases (whether knowingly granted by host countries or not) and changes in alliances between nonstate organizations and their state allies are important factors in the decline of terrorism. Syrian relationships with Palestinian and Lebanese factions clearly matter, as do Iranian relationships with Shi'ite opposition movements in Lebanon and Kuwait. As mentioned earlier, Western press accounts attributed the decline in terrorism in Western Europe after 1985 (a high point) to East European restrictions on the movements of Middle Eastern groups.

In contrast, James Adams argues that West European

cooperation turned the tide in the combat against the terrorist underground.[51] Aggressive law enforcement worked, according to his analysis. After 1986, greater information-sharing among European states, based on computer data banks that could technically be linked to each other, was an important advance. Terrorist mobility has been restricted, intelligence services have made terrorism a top priority, and governments are working to cut off the financial resources available to terrorists. It is likely, however, that indigenous terrorism in Western Europe had already begun to decline.

Controlling terrorism is not an important policy issue for governments not currently threatened. Here one may note the importance of persuading governments to view their security interests as long term rather than short term. Convincing presently unaffected states not only that their assistance is necessary but that cooperation is actually in their future interest is essential to success, especially since cooperation is costly. Arguments for cooperation should be based on analysis of the conditions under which terrorism spreads, such as, for example, contagion processes. The growth of ideologies hostile to both the West and the Soviet Union is one factor; for example, Sendero Luminoso in Peru is fanatically Maoist and opposes the present governments of both the Soviet Union and China, as well as the United States. Religious extremism in the Middle East is coupled with nationalism in a volatile mixture that could inspire opposition in multiethnic states such as the Soviet Union. Domestic liberalization in the Soviet Union, including tolerance of dissent and press coverage of violence (for example, in Azerbaijan), may create a permissive environment for domestic terrorism, while Armenian discontent may furnish a powerful motive. Assassinations and assassination attempts have occurred in Hungary and Yugoslavia, as well as in the West.

The benefits of cooperation are not restricted to reducing terrorism. Powerful states seeking cooperation possess the resources to furnish both tangible and intangible rewards for cooperative behavior. Most states value their international reputations, and cooperation against terrorism could increase

---

51. James Adams, "The End of the Reign of Terrorism," *The Washington Post National Weekly Edition*, February 29-March 6, 1988, p. 23.

national prestige. The West is able to offer economic rewards as well. Rather than treating terrorism as a separate issue, states could make deals across issues.

Another potential benefit for East-West cooperation against terrorism lies in the area of general confidence-building.[52] This benefit is costless and presumably equally valuable to all parties. The issue of terrorism has become such a distinctive symbol of distrust that even limited agreement would have a positive impact.

For cooperation to work, its long-term payoff must be shown to be greater than the immediate reward of giving in to terrorists' demands or not restricting their movements. (Although it is easier to understand the value of making concessions in order to secure the freedom of hostages than it is to see what is to be gained by seeking the goodwill of or influence over the shadowy undergrounds that most often use terrorism.) It is essential to recognize that there are concrete liabilities to cooperation. Here also important questions remain unanswered. In the short run, does a conciliatory position provide immunity from terrorism? For example, the West German refusal to extradite Mohammed Ali Hamadi to the United States was said to be motivated in part by fear of reprisals. France was said to be unwilling to offend Syria by agreeing to British demands for sanctions because Syrian help was needed to release French hostages in Lebanon. French nationals became the targets of Basque terrorism when France began extraditing ETA suspects to Spain.

Rewards for cooperation must be designed to outweigh other costs as well. Generally the issue of economic sanctions comes up against various sorts of economic dependencies between West European and Middle Eastern states. West Europeans have also feared the political consequences of being associated with what they see as U.S. irresponsibility or monolithic anti-Communism, the "simplistic activism" Brzezinski decries. Distinguishing opposition to terrorism from opposition to Communism would reduce the risks of cooperation for many states.

---

52. See, for example, the paper by Robert Garai of the Hungarian Institute of International Relations, Budapest, presented to the conference on International Aspects of Terrorism (fn. 28).

■ Penalties for Noncooperation

The costs associated with uncooperative policies go beyond the issue of directly controlling terrorism: alienating domestic and international public opinion, losing international reputation and incurring the displeasure of other states that value cooperation. Powerful states that desire cooperation can make passive noncooperation as well as aggressive defiance of the rules painful by applying economic, diplomatic and even military sanctions.

The 1986 U.S. raid against Libya is an interesting example of how punitive sanctions work with regard to different forms of noncooperation. European unwillingness to agree to diplomatic and economic sanctions against Libya influenced the U.S. decision to retaliate, just as reluctance to impose sanctions against Iran was a factor in U.S. President Jimmy Carter's attempt at a military rescue in Iran in 1980. The bombing raid was a form of direct punishment of Libya, but its effectiveness depended more on Western Europe than Libya. Whether or not it actually deterred Libya from giving further assistance to terrorist factions is difficult to determine. However, the raid demonstrated to the United States' reluctant allies that frustration would lead to the use of military force and to agreement on stricter anti-terrorist measures. Adam Roberts, Professor of International Relations at Oxford, noted that "the very threat of international disorder implicit in the April 1986 US raid on Libya may, paradoxically, have spurred other states to take the matter of nonviolent sanctions more seriously—which they did, for example at the Tokyo summit."[53]

The destabilizing consequences of military reactions exceed those of terrorism. One effect of the 1986 bombing was increased opposition to military retaliation. Thus in December 1988, after the bombing of a Pan Am flight, the United Kingdom quickly stated that retaliation would be inappropriate. Escalation of regional conflict is a major risk. The 1970 Jordanian civil war, precipitated by the hijackings of the PFLP, threatened to draw in Syria and Israel, and with them their respective superpower allies.

Another harmful consequence of noncooperation is that

---

53. Adam Roberts, "Terrorism and International Order," in Lawrence Freedman, et al., *Terrorism and International Order*, p. 22. See also Putnam and Bayne, *Hanging Together*, pp. 212–213.

states victimized by terrorism will turn to extended covert operations. The recent U.K. killing of three unarmed IRA members in Gibraltar may signal such a trend. It should be remembered that in the 1970s, Israeli frustration led to the establishment of a special intelligence unit to track down and assassinate suspected Black September activists in Europe.

■ Distinguishing Cooperation from Defection

Cooperation cannot be rewarded or noncooperation punished unless states can determine when rules are being broken. An important aspect of establishing penalties for noncooperation is distinguishing types of defection. There are three fundamental kinds of noncooperation. The first, a highly visible form of noncooperation, involves failure to agree to or to implement anti-terrorist measures that the majority of states support, such as economic or diplomatic sanctions against states that aid terrorists. Such passive noncooperation may also involve refusals to extradite persons suspected of terrorism. Failure to improve airport security also falls into this category. Within the European Community, for example, Greece has frequently been criticized for these reasons. An Italian request for extradition was rejected in 1988. Both Greece and Spain resisted explicit references to Libya in Community condemnations of terrorism. States that fail to implement sanctions, improve security or extradite suspected terrorists are regarded as injuring the interests of states that do cooperate. In particular, the countries that do not agree to sanctions may profit economically, moving in to take over areas of trade and commerce that the cooperators have voluntarily renounced.

A second type of noncooperation involves making deals with extremist organizations, to secure either the release of hostages or the immunity of one's home territory or nationals. This policy area is both highly complex and secretive, and thus defection is difficult to detect. Deals may be struck with the states which sponsor or influence undergrounds, in which case payoffs can be disguised as normalization of relationships or rewards for helpfulness. Deals may also be made directly with the nonstate organizations that are the primary actors in the process of terrorism. In this case, the risk of deception is high, and governments are often swindled when financial payoffs are involved. Either type of deal can be made directly, by government agents, or through private intermediaries. This type of noncooperation is harmful to the international community if the users of terrorism are either encouraged to continue terrorism in the hopes of future payoffs or provided the financial resources necessary to subsidize further terrorist activities.

The last type of defection is the most serious and also the most unusual since it concerns state sponsorship of terrorism. Yet assigning responsibility for terrorism is often impossible. Even if a government has reasonably well-grounded suspicions about state involvement, constraints on revealing sensitive intelligence information can prevent its public dissemination. Having to retract charges can also be embarrassing. For example, the bombing of the La Belle discotheque in West Berlin originally traced to Libya has now been linked to Syria. States that assist terrorist organizations are usually careful to conceal their involvement. Nor is it easy to be precise about what aiding terrorists means. How can an observer distinguish, for example, between training camps for terrorists and training camps for "national liberation" organizations, or between weapons that can be used for insurgency and those that are convenient for terrorism? Nevertheless some examples of this type of defection are quite blatant. In 1986, the Republic of Ireland discovered an IRA arms cache marked "Libyan Armed Forces," containing AK47 assault rifles made in East Germany and Romania and ammunition from Yugoslavia.

Even if the rules for cooperation were precisely defined, the mutual benefits of cooperation and the costs of failure explicitly recognized, and ways found to distinguish between cooperation and defection, states would not always be able to control their ability to cooperate. Internal and bureaucratic factors often complicate unilateral responses to terrorism as well as cooperative policies. Domestic pressures can seriously decrease control over foreign policy decisions. The U.S. government, for example, was forced to negotiate at length with congressional leaders in order to secure Senate approval of the 1986 supplemental extradition treaty with the United Kingdom. The result was a compromise. The Libya raid also elicited objections from some members of the U.S. Congress who felt that the use of military force against terrorism should be subject to the provisions of the War Powers Act, which requires executive consultation with the legislature before U.S. forces are engaged in situations where hostilities are imminent as well as legislative approval for a continuation of a military deployment beyond sixty days. Similarly, the Iran-Contra affair resulted not only in congressional criticism of the Reagan Administration and a loss of popular support for the presidency, but also in criminal indictments for the Administration officials responsible. Similar considerations explain the policies of other states. Apparently in 1984 the issue of terrorism arose at short notice at the London summit because Prime Minister Thatcher was concerned about a summit declaration that would pacify U.K. public opinion after the killing of a policewoman outside the Libyan People's Bureau in London's St. James Square.

The implications of the Iran-Contra affair also cast doubt on the feasibility of a consistent no-concessions policy as part of a structure of international cooperation. Government leaders may feel compelled to take action to secure the release of hostages, whether because they feel personally obligated, sense the pressure of public opinion or fear a repetition of the first Iranian crisis with its disastrous political consequences for President Carter. The no-concessions posture was tenable only in rhetoric, and rigid public insistence on its absolute applicability not only to U.S. policy but to that of West European governments forced some members of the Reagan Administration into covert deals to free American hostages in Lebanon. Yet making deals with terrorists may appear unsavory and opportunistic to the public, especially if obviously linked to electoral considerations.

5

Nuclear Terrorism: A Case Study

An area in which concern over risks is mounting and which also holds a promise for closer East-West cooperation is the prospect of terrorist exploitation of nuclear power, whether through theft or construction of a nuclear explosive device, dissemination of plutonium or radioactive material, or attacks on nuclear power facilities. Both civil and military nuclear programs are vulnerable. In 1986, Soviet General Secretary Gorbachev submitted a statement to the United Nations calling for a reliable system of measures to prevent nuclear terrorism. The issue was also raised by the Soviet Union at a special session on Chernobyl of the International Atomic Energy Agency (IAEA). In the United States the Nuclear Control Institute, a private organization, recently issued a report calling attention to the problem.[54] Title V of the 1986 Omnibus Diplomatic Security and Antiterrorism Act deals with international nuclear terrorism. A report from the Department of Defense required by that legislation warned that, as the commercial use of plutonium increases (by the late 1990s, 300 shipments of plutonium are expected to leave Europe annually), so do the opportunities for terrorism.[55]

Recognition of the possibility that two lines of technical

---

54. The International Task Force report is published in Paul L. Leventhal and Yonah Alexander, eds., *Preventing Nuclear Terrorism* (Lexington, MA: Lexington Books, 1987), pp. 7–44. A useful summary of the report and its background studies can be found in Paul L. Leventhal and Milton M. Hoenig, "The Hidden Danger: Risks of Nuclear Terrorism," *Terrorism: An International Journal* 10 (1987), pp. 1–22. For Gorbachev's position, see the background paper by George Bunn, "International Arrangements against Nuclear Terrorism," p. 354.
55. *The New York Times*, November 5, 1987, p. A5.

and political development might intersect—the proliferation of civilian and military nuclear power and the growth in terrorism—dates from the early 1970s.[56] Although the nuclear threat had not then and has not now materialized, there is no doubt that the terrorist use of any form of nuclear device or even credible blackmail would have a formidable impact on government policies and public thinking about nuclear power. Thus, although the likelihood of such an event seemed small, preventive measures were implemented on domestic and international levels. The question is whether enough has been done to promote adequate nuclear security, even within the United States. A study by the Nuclear Policy Program at the University of California, Santa Cruz, finds that the U.S. Nuclear Regulatory Commission underestimates the threat.[57] This study contends that the assumptions upon which the security policies of the 1970s were based are now false. Truck bombs, in particular, were not foreseen at the time. Terrorist groups are no longer restricted in terms of capabilities or constrained by moral or political compunctions from causing mass civilian casualties. The primary intent of terrorism is to outrage, and organizations willing to explode bombs that kill hundreds of airline passengers or demolish buildings cannot be said to be inhibited from causing fatalities. Furthermore, nuclear power plants can suffer severe core damage more easily than was previously thought. The disasters at Three Mile Island and Chernobyl have brought this lesson home. These unanticipated accidents make the destruction of civilian reactors a credible terrorist threat.

In response to such concerns, the International Task Force on Prevention of Nuclear Terrorism was convened in 1985 and commissioned a series of background papers analyzing the terrorist threat and strategies for dealing with it. Its final report concludes that while the risk is still low, "the interest of terrorists to acquire nuclear weapons should be regarded as technically, politically, and psychologically plausible."[58] The

---

56. For a collection of articles on the subject, see Augustus R. Norton and Martin H. Greenberg, eds., *Studies in Nuclear Terrorism* (Boston: G.K. Hall, 1979).
57. Daniel Hirsch, Stephanie Murphy and Bennett Ramberg, "Protecting Reactors from Terrorists," *Bulletin of the Atomic Scientists* 42 (March 1986), pp. 22–25.
58. Leventhal and Alexander, *Preventing Nuclear Terrorism*, p. xii.

confluence of a number of factors—growing sophistication and destructiveness of terrorism; evidence of state support; deployment of nuclear weapons in areas of intense terrorist activity, such as West Germany or Italy; proliferation; and vulnerability of civil nuclear programs—creates unprecedented opportunities for disruption. The Task Force findings emphasize that Western Europe, which according to the State Department suffered the highest number of international terrorist attacks between 1970 and 1985, is second in the world in intensity of nuclear development (4,800 battlefield nuclear weapons at 123 different NATO sites; 1,100 French and British weapons; and 340 civil or military nuclear facilities).

The incentives for cooperation against nuclear terrorism are high precisely because of the potentially catastrophic consequences of such high-technology terrorism. Even a hoax could create widespread public panic and precipitate overreaction on the part of a threatened government. The use of a nuclear device by a non-state organization in the context of a regional conflict would intensify the risk of escalation. The fact that nuclear reactors have already been attacked in the Middle East may signal an erosion of inhibitions. If there were suspicions of state involvement in an act of nuclear terrorism, reactions would be swift and forceful. Similarly, were chemical weapons to be used for terrorist purposes, the pressure to retaliate would likely be irresistible. Iraq's use of chemical weapons and potential Libyan acquisition of a production capability are ominous developments.

In contrast to other forms of terrorism, the nuclear area is one in which a substantial foundation of international cooperation already exists, primarily because of the links between the issues of terrorism, arms control and nonproliferation.[59] This state of affairs is encouraging for the future because the rules of cooperation are well developed, cooperation is institutionalized and the benefits of cooperation are generally recognized. The superpowers have a mutual interest in prevention. The issue has not yet become politicized. The existing international nonproliferation regime, which is supported by both the United States and the Soviet Union, probably contributes most

---

59. See George Bunn, "International Arrangements," in Leventhal and Alexander, *Preventing Nuclear Terrorism.*

to limiting terrorist opportunities. Its centerpiece is the 1968 Non-Proliferation Treaty (NPT) under which its non-nuclear weapons state adherents agree to accept IAEA inspections. In 1980 under IAEA auspices the Convention on the Physical Protection of Nuclear Materials applied security standards to the international transport and storage of nuclear materials. The Convention, which has been ratified by both the United States and the Soviet Union, came into force in 1987. It requires its signatories to pass domestic legislation mandating prosecution or extradition of nuclear terrorists.

The issue of civilian nuclear exports has also been the subject of informal East-West cooperation. In 1974, after the Indian explosion of a nuclear device, a Nuclear Suppliers' Group (the "London Club") met to develop guidelines for export security, which were submitted to the IAEA in 1978. These guidelines do not constitute a binding international treaty, but they are observed as national policies. The Suppliers' Group linked U.S. and Soviet interests, as well as those of both East and West European nuclear exporters. Cooperation has resulted in the exercise of restraint in nuclear transfers as well as the adherence to mutually agreed upon guidelines when transfers are made. In this issue-area, more disputes have occurred among Western states (between the United States and West Germany, for example, over sales to Third World states) than between East and West.

In addition, direct U.S.-Soviet cooperation to prevent a nuclear crisis from accidentally triggering a superpower confrontation is underway, although these discussions remain extremely confidential. In 1984, the upgrade of the hotline between the United States and the Soviet Union added facsimile capabilities and more rapid communications links, and in 1985 the Standing Consultative Commission announced an understanding on the 1971 Accidents Measures Agreement that apparently clarified U.S. and Soviet responsibilities should a non-state actor instigate a nuclear explosion. The terms of the agreement remain secret.

The original concept of the Nuclear Risk Reduction Centers (established in September 1987) was proposed by Senators Sam Nunn and John Warner, who persuaded first the U.S. Administration and then Gorbachev to support the idea. The proposal was strongly oriented toward the prevention of a superpower conflict resulting from nuclear terrorism.[60] Their 1983 report noted a "rising danger of nuclear terrorism." Subsequent legislation called for the exchange of information, discussion of procedures to be followed during possible incidents, and maintenance of contact during threats or incidents. Senators Nunn and Warner also suggested that the risk reduction centers serve as the location for a standing working group on nuclear terrorism as well as for regular high-level meetings to discuss joint procedures in the event of nuclear terrorism.

The Reagan Administration, however, favored a much less ambitious concept, focusing strictly on prevention rather than crisis management. Thus the Risk Reduction Centers were not assigned a role in contingency planning for future incidents of nuclear terrorism. In 1987, the U.S. and the USSR signed an agreement establishing the centers, with a second hotline. The agreement was regarded as a promising first step and useful confidence-building measure, even though the results were more modest than Senators Nunn and Warner had originally hoped. Barry M. Blechman concludes that these were useful if minor measures to reduce the risk of inadvertent conflict: "Carrying out such discussion in normal times could help allay suspicions on the two sides, develop bureaucratic routines that might facilitate cooperation in unknown contingencies, and also build confidence in the efficacy of this technical channel, enabling it to be used to help manage crises." Should there be an incident of nuclear terrorism, "the centers could provide the means for experts, working under the direction of national leaders, to communicate important technical and operational information rapidly and comprehensively. Although the centers would not be used to resolve the substantive aspects of great power confrontations, they could provide a means of supplementing diplomatic exchanges with technical expertise."[61]

---

60. Sam Nunn and John W. Warner, "U.S.-Soviet Cooperation in Countering Nuclear Terrorism: The Role of Risk Reduction Centers," pp. 381–393 in Leventhal and Alexander, *Preventing Nuclear Terrorism*. See also *The New York Times*, September 16, 1987, p. 1.
61. Barry M. Blechman, "Efforts to Reduce the Risk of Accidental or Inadvertent War," in Alexander L. George, Philip J. Farley and Alexander Dallin, eds., *U.S.-Soviet Security Cooperation: Achievements, Failures, Lessons* (New York: Oxford University Press, 1988), p. 477.

A rather more comprehensive agenda of recommended government actions has been offered by the Task Force on Prevention of Nuclear Terrorism, which mentions 51 concrete measures to reduce the risk of theft of military weapons and reactor fuels, protect civilian powerplants, improve the capabilities of intelligence services and expand U.S.-Soviet cooperation. Securing universal adherence to the Convention on the Physical Protection of Nuclear Materials is a general priority. Its provisions do not yet extend to domestic transport, use and storage of special nuclear materials, which are covered by IAEA regulations that may be in need of review. Many authorities have also suggested holding international conferences such as, for example, an IAEA experts' conference on the protection of nuclear materials from terrorists or a comprehensive review of the problem of nuclear terrorism. International efforts beyond safeguarding may be required, such as bans on reprocessing nuclear fuel. Stockpiling plutonium and highly enriched uranium is dangerous with or without safeguards. In 1986, Congress called on the president to seek agreement in the UN Security Council to establish an effective regime of international sanctions against violations of agreements on safeguards and to propose measures for a coordinated international response.

Controlling the spread of nuclear weapons would assist in preventing terrorism. The association between high levels of destructiveness and state support is not coincidental. What are the barriers to cooperation in the nuclear area? The secrecy that surrounds nuclear weapons issues may complicate agreement (such as removing battlefield weapons from areas of endemic terrorism), but the arms control area is an encouraging precedent. Issues of sovereignty arise when international arrangements intrude into domestic jurisdictions over civilian nuclear facilities, as is the case with safeguard requirements, especially inspections. The non-nuclear weapons states may resent efforts to control their behavior in the absence of superpower arms control agreements. The interest of some near-nuclear states (such as Pakistan) in acquiring nuclear capabilities, for instance, has not diminished despite American disapproval. Economic incentives for civilian nuclear exports are strong. There is also some fear that publicizing the possibility of nuclear terrorism will give the idea to potential offenders.

6

Conclusions

In 1986, the Vice President's Task Force on Combatting Terrorism called international cooperation "the first line of defense" and "the best hope for long-term success" against terrorism.[62] The pursuit of cooperation requires that the U.S. government develop a pragmatic approach to the subject of terrorism, a balanced analytical perspective that neither inflates nor minimizes the importance of the threat terrorism poses to national and international security. Conceptions of both security and terrorism must be clarified and explained. The use of the term as a pejorative label in foreign policy or as a debating point in domestic politics should be avoided. In return, the United States can expect the East to refrain from rhetorical denunciations of U.S. imperialism and "state terrorism" or other comments that might be construed, however erroneously, as justification for anti-American violence. Mutual restraint is an important starting point for discussions.

The U.S. interest in cooperation lies principally in two areas: controlling the real danger of terrorism by preventing its occurrence and limiting its damage, and developing a system of effective collective management of international security problems. The pursuit of cooperation against terrorism should not be based on an insistence that all policies that benefit the United States necessarily benefit all other states. Nations differ in their vulnerabilities and response capabilities. The United States cannot simply ask others to endorse American national policies. Cooperation has to be negotiated, not imposed. The

---

62. The text of the public report is contained in *International Terrorism* (fn. 25), pp. 793–826. See especially p. 806.

purpose of cooperation is to improve international security by building on national strengths, not to produce uniform policies. The United States is the favorite target of international terrorism but suffers little violence on national territory. The situation is the reverse for many other states, including those of Western Europe and Latin America. Other states have enjoyed a relative immunity. These differences in situation cannot be ignored. However, they can form the basis for functional differentiation in the struggle against terrorism.

If the United States is to maintain the lead in promoting cooperation against terrorism, national policy must not succumb to short-term interests or domestic pressures. At the same time, American policymakers must be sensitive to the domestic preoccupations of other states. The appearance of selfishness and hypocrisy—a result of the Iran-*Contra* affair and also, unfairly, of the drive for economic sanctions against Libya— must be avoided if others are to be persuaded to see their interests as long term. Policy credibility is a priority. It is also important to avoid the appearance of military adventurism or crusades against particular states or leaders. Support for terrorism, not aggressive rhetoric, should be punished.

An important lesson for future cooperation is that discussions of the issue must be well prepared. The Western summit treatment of terrorism often suffered because it was an ad hoc reaction to events. Discussions resulted in dramatic declarations without practical follow up. If a consensus is to be both reached and carried out, careful advance planning is required. Governments have available to them extensive expertise on terrorism, much of which remains underutilized. This body of expertise goes beyond accumulating facts to interpreting terrorism and explaining its relationship to national and international security. Multilateral initiatives must be founded on comprehensive and objective analysis of the problem.

Perhaps the most important way in which international cooperation can control terrorism and limit state support is through public exposure. States that aid terrorist undergrounds do not want to be caught. If they were willing to be held accountable for their behavior, they would not resort to concealment behind ephemeral and shadowy extremist organizations. The Syrian reaction to British and European Community sanctions in 1986 is a case in point. The collective assignment of responsibility for terrorism would be an effective form of international censure.

A pragmatic approach should focus on isolating terrorism as an unacceptable activity regardless of the political cause it purports to express. The point should be made and repeated that no cause is well served by terrorism, which can only fail as a means of bringing about long-term political change. Terrorism is most often damaging to the hopes of those who use it, not only because it provokes government repression but because terrorism unites the public against it and in support of a hard-line response. Terrorism should be discredited as a method, but it is pointless to deny that ambiguities exist in defining it and distinguishing it from other forms of violence. Yet at the core of terrorism is its direct challenge to the state's monopoly on the use of force, its claim to command the loyalty and obedience of its citizens, and hence to its legitimacy. On the international level, terrorism involves deliberate defiance of the accepted norms of civilized behavior. It is not common crime, nor is it a necessary component of the revolutionary process. Understanding the phenomenon also requires the recognition that terrorism is context-dependent. The users of terrorism depend on exploiting political conflicts that furnish motives and justifications for violence. Dismissing inquiry into the causes of terrorism as an attempt to excuse it is short-sighted.

Expectations of what can be achieved through policy changes, whether unilateral or multilateral, must be both clear and modest. Terrorism can at best be reduced but not eradicated. There is no magic solution and no absolute security. Terrorism is inherently difficult to prevent because much activity is the work of small autonomous underground factions attacking targets of opportunity. Terrorism is used precisely because it is cheap and easy. These unstable, weakly organized groups will not be easy to control. It will thus be extremely important, should cooperation proceed, that U.S. aspirations not be inflated, leading to disappointment and suspicion when terrorism does not vanish. However, it is realistic to expect strengthened international cooperation to have general benefits, in bringing about improved understanding of the issue and greater mutual trust. It is also possible that East-West cooperation could strengthen Western cooperation, as Europeans need no longer fear that they are being pressured into joining a U.S. anti-Communist crusade. The attractiveness of the alternative of unilateral military intervention would surely be lessened if the United States were assured of helpful reactions not only from friends but from adversaries. The mere fact of explicit East-West agreement that terrorism is an affront to all states would be reassuring to its victims and discouraging to its advocates.

After the development of a common understanding of the problem of terrorism, progress toward cooperation requires that the United States be prepared to reward cooperation and punish noncooperation. Careful consideration should be given to the twin problems of defining cooperation and detecting violations of cooperative obligations. Threats to punish state support of terrorism that can neither be discovered nor exposed result only in loss of credibility. Methods of reward and punishment that are both flexible and feasible are needed. Military retaliation is a dangerous way of frightening one's allies into cooperation, and its effectiveness as a deterrent to aggression is undetermined. Substitutes should be found. It would be well to remember the importance of prestige and reputation as values in international relations. Diplomatic embarrassment can motivate cooperation. This requirement also means that the United States should acknowledge the costs of cooperation and try to find practical yet subtle ways of offsetting them. For example, extraditing accused terrorists according to U.S. request increases the vulnerability of the cooperative state. The costs of implementing sanctions against Libya, Syria or Iran are probably greater for Europe than for the United States. Europeans value an independent foreign policy. It is difficult to convince states to undertake an action that is directly painful to them for the sake of an uncertain future reward.

The appropriate forum for East-West discussions of the issue would be regular meetings, either summits or working groups at lower levels of government. In such a context terrorism could be discussed informally without attracting the excessive publicity that arouses expectations and generates pressures to score debating points. It seems likely that a specialized high-level conference devoted exclusively to terrorism, whether or not in the context of the United Nations, would suffer from these defects, but the presence of terrorism as one item on a larger agenda or the establishment of informal working groups would not. Nor is it necessarily wise to elevate the significance of terrorism unnecessarily. It is not the most important policy problem facing the superpowers. Moreover, excessive public attention to the issue plays into the hands of the weak but disruptive actors whose only source of power lies in how the rest of the world reacts to them. Discussions of terrorism should become a normal and unexceptional part of East-West relations.

What cooperative measures might profitably be discussed in such a framework? Issues that provoke dissension among Western allies or that are unenforceable had best be left to national discretion for the time being. Automatic extradition and universal no-concessions policies fall into this category. Items that could be placed on the agenda include:

- facilitation of bilateral exchanges of information about terrorism, especially timely warning of planned attacks or notification of intended responses, by creating both a favorable climate of opinion and appropriate procedures;

- refusal of military, financial or logistical assistance (safe haven or border transit privileges) to any non-state organization, whatever its ideological leaning, that relies on terrorist attacks on civilians, especially those actions that endanger civil aviation or the conduct of diplomacy, or that involve the seizure of hostages;

- public denunciations of deliberate attacks on civilians or hostage-takings, without exception as to motive or situation;

- agreement in principle that diplomatic facilities should not be used as bases for organizing clandestine violence;

- restrictions on arms sales, particularly transfers of explosives and weapons used for terrorism, to states that do not restrict their dissemination; and

- a joint declaration calling for universal ratification and implementation of the existing multilateral anti-terrorist conventions.

Effective international cooperation has to be based on a mutuality of interest. Both the United States and the Soviet Union have a strong interest in a stable international system. Failure to cooperate to control terrorism is risky. Not only is there the likelihood that uncurbed terrorism will increase in scope and destructiveness, perhaps even to the extent of nuclear or chemical threats, but also that frustration will compel states to resort to military force in order to preempt or retaliate, resulting in unintentional escalation to regional or global conflict. The precedent of World War I should not be ignored. No contemporary observers thought that Austria's desire to punish Serbia for aiding nationalist terrorism would precipitate world war. The problem of how to respond to terrorism has divided the West from the East, from the Third World and within itself. A temporary and probably superficial unity in the Western alliance was reached only in the troubled aftermath of a military expression of U.S. anger. Unilateralism will remain the preference of the United States until it can be demonstrated that multilateral solutions can be reached. Terrorism is a persistent source of international disorder, and the problem of how to control it should be routinely considered in the context of general U.S.-Soviet security cooperation.

Appendix
Key Documents on Terrorism
1978-1989

Document 1

International Convention Against The Taking of Hostages

The States Parties to this Convention, December 17, 1979

Having in mind the purposes and principles of the Charter of the United Nations concerning the maintenance of international peace and security and the promotion of friendly relations and co-operating among States,

Recognizing in particular that everyone has right to life, liberty and security of person, as set out in the Universal Declaration of Human Rights and the International Covenant on Civil and Political Rights,

Reaffirming the principle of equal rights and self-determination of peoples as enshrined in the Charter of the United Nations and the Declaration on Principles of International Law concerning Friendly Relations and Co-operation among States in accordance with the Charter of the United Nations, as well as in other relevant resolutions of the General Assembly,

Considering that the taking of hostages is an offence of grave concern to the international community and that, in accordance with the provisions of this Convention, any person committing an act of hostage taking shall either be prosecuted or extradited.

Being convinced that it is urgently necessary to develop international co-operation between States in devising and adopting effective measures for the prevention, prosecution and punishment of all acts of taking of hostages as manifestations of international terrorism,

Have agreed as follows:

Article 1

1. Any person who seizes or detains and threatens to kill, to injure or to continue to detain another person (hereinafter referred to as the "hostage") in order to compel a third party, namely, a State, an international intergovernmental organization, a natural or juridical person, or a group of persons, to do or abstain from doing any act as an explicit or implicit condition for the release of the hostage commits the offence of taking hostages ("hostage-taking") within the meaning of this Covention.

2. Any person who:

(a) attempts to commit an act of hostage-taking, or

(b) participates as an accomplice of anyone who commits or attempts to commit an act of hostage-taking likewise commits an offence for the purposes of this Convention.

Article 2

Each State Party shall make the offences set forth in article 1 punishable by appropriate penalties which take into account the grave nature of those offences.

Article 3

1. The State Party in the territory of which the hostage is held by the offender shall take all measures it considers appropriate to ease the situation of the hostage, in particular, to secure his release and, after his release, to facilitate, when relevant, his departure.

2. If any object which the offender has obtained as a result of the taking of hostages comes into the custody of a State Party, that State Party shall return it as soon as possible to the hostage or the third party referred to in article 1, as the case may be, or to the appropriate authorities thereof.

Article 4

States Parties shall co-operate in the prevention of the offences set forth in article 1, particularly by:

(a) taking all practicable measures to prevent preparations in their respective territories for the commission of those offences within or outside their territories, including measures to prohibit in their territories illegal activities of persons, groups and organizations that encourage, instigate, organize or engage in the perpetration of acts of taking of hostages;

(b) exchanging information and co-ordinating the taking of administrative and other measures as appropriate to prevent the commission of those offences.

Article 5

1. Each State Party shall take such measures as may be necessary to establish its jurisdiction over any of the offences set forth in article 1 which are committed:

(a) in its territory or on board a ship or aircraft registered in that State;

(b) by any of its nationals, or, if the State considers it appropriate, by those stateless persons who have their habitual residence in its territory;

(c) in order to compel that State to do or abstain from doing any act; or

(d) with respect to a hostage who is a national of that State, if that State considers it appropriate.

2. Each State Party shall likewise take such measures as may be necessary to establish its jurisdiction over the offences set forth in article 1 in cases where the alleged offender is present in its territory and it does not extradite him to any of the States mentioned in paragraph 1 of this article.

3. This Convention does not exclude any criminal jursidiction exercised in accordance with internal law.

Article 6

1. Upon being satisfied that the circumstances so warrant, any State Party in the Territory of which the alleged offender is present shall, in accordance with its laws, take him into custody or take other measures to ensure his presence for such time as is necessary to enable any criminal or extradition proceedings to be instituted. That State Party shall immediately make a preliminary inquiry into the facts.

2. The custody or other measures referred to in paragraph 1 of this article shall be notified without delay directly or through the Secretary-General of the United Nations to:

(a) the State where the offense was committed;

(b) the State against which compulsion has been directed or attempted;

(c) the State of which the natural or juridical person against whom compulsion has been directed or attempted is a national;

(d) the State of which the hostage is a national or in the territory of which he has his habitual residence;

(e) the State of which the alleged offender is a national or, if he is a stateless person, in the territory of which he has his habitual residence;

(f) the international intergovernmental organization against which compulsion has been directed or attempted;

(g) all other states concerned.

3. Any person regarding whom the measures referred to in paragraph 1 of this article are being taken shall be entitled:

(a) to communicate without delay with the nearest appropriate representative of the State of which he is a national or which is otherwise entitled to establish such communication or, if he is a stateless person, the State in the territory of which he has his habitual residence;

(b) to be visited by a representative of that State.

4. The rights referred to in paragraph 3 of this article shall be exercised in conformity with the laws and regulations of the State in the territory of which the alleged offender is present subject to the proviso, however, that the said laws and regulations must enable full effect to be given to the purposes for which the rights accorded under paragraph 3 of this article are intended.

5. The provisions of paragraphs 3 and 4 of this article shall be without prejudice to the right of any State Party having a claim to jurisdiction in accordance with paragraph 1(b) of article 5 to invite the International Committee of the Red Cross to communicate with and visit the alleged offender.

6. The State which makes the preliminary inquiry contemplated in paragraph 1 of this article shall promptly report its findings to the States or organization referred to in paragraph 2 of this article and indicate whether it intends to exercise jurisdiction.

Article 7

The State Party where the alleged offender is prosecuted shall in accordance with its laws communicate the final outcome of the proceedings to the Secretary-General of the United Nations, who shall transmit the information to the other States concerned and the international intergovernmental organizations concerned.

Article 8

1. The State Party in the territory of which the alleged offender is found shall, if it does not extradite him, be obliged, without exception whatsoever and whether or not the offence was committed in its territory, to submit the case to its competent authorities for the purpose of prosecution, through proceedings in accordance with the laws of that State. Those authorities shall take their decision in the same manner as in the case of any ordinary offence of a grave nature under the law of that State.

2. Any person regarding whom proceedings are being carried out in connexion with any of the offences set forth in article 1 shall be guaranteed fair treatment at all stages of the proceedings, including enjoyment of all the rights and guarantees provided by the law of the State in the territory of which he is present.

Article 9

1. A request for the extradition of an alleged offender, pursuant to this Convention, shall not be granted if the requested State Party has substantial grounds for believing:

(a) that the request for extradition for an offence set forth in article 1 has been made for the purpose of prosecuting or punishing a person on account of his race, religion, nationality, ethnic origin or political opinion; or

(b) that the person's position may be prejudiced:

(i) for any of the reasons mentioned in subparagraph (a) of this paragraph, or

(ii) for the reason that communication with him by the appropriate authorities of the State entitled to exercise rights of protection cannot be effected.

2. With respect to the offences as defined in this Convention, the provisions of all extradition treaties and arrangements applicable between States Parties are modified as between States Parties to the extent that they are incompatible with this Convention.

Article 10

1. The offences set forth in article 1 shall be deemed to be included as extraditable offences in any extradition treaty existing between States Parties. States Parties undertake to include such offences as extraditable offences in every extradition treaty to be concluded between them.

2. If a State Party which makes extradition conditional on the existence of a treaty receives a request for extradition from another State Party with which it has no extradition treaty, the requested State may at its option consider this Convention as the legal basis for extradition in respect of the offences set forth in article 1. Extradition shall be subject to the other conditions provided by the law of the requested State.

3. State Parties which do not make extradition conditional on the existence of a treaty shall recognize the offences set forth in article 1 as extraditable offences between themselves subject to the conditions provided by the law of the requested State.

4. The offences set forth in article 1 shall be treated, for the purpose of extradition between States Parties, as if they had been committed not only in the place in which they occurred but also in the territories of the States required to establish their jurisdiction in accordance with paragraph 1 of article 5.

Article 11

1. States Parties shall afford one another the greatest measure of assistance in connexion with criminal proceedings brought in respect of the offences set forth in article 1, including the supply of all evidence at their disposal necessary for the proceedings.

2. The provisions of paragraph 1 of this article shall not affect obligations concerning mutual judicial assistance embodied in any other treaty.

Article 12

In so far as the Geneva Conventions of 1949 for the protection of war victims or the Protocols Additional to those Conventions are applicable to a particular act of hostage-taking, and in so far as States Parties to this Convention are bound under those conventions to prosecute or hand over the hostage-taker, the present Convention shall not apply to an act of hostage-taking committed in the course of armed conflicts as defined in the Geneva Conventions of 1949 and the Protocols thereto, including armed conflicts mentioned in article 1, paragraph 4, Additional Protocol I of 1977, in which peoples are fighting against colonial domination and alien occupation and against racist regimes in the exercise of their right of self-determination, as enshrined in the Charter of the United Nations and the Declaration on Principles of International Law concerning Friendly Relations and Co-operation among States in accordance with the Charter of the United Nations.

Article 13

This Convention shall not apply where the offence is committed within a single State, the hostage and the alleged offender are nationals of that State and the alleged offender is found in the territory of that State.

Article 14

Nothing in this Convention shall be construed as justifying the violation of the territorial integrity or political independence of a State in contravention of the Charter of the United Nations.

Article 15

The provisions of this Convention shall not affect the application of the Treaties on Asylum, in force at the date of the adoption of this Convention, as between the States which are parties to those Treaties; but a State Party to this Convention may not invoke those Treaties with respect to another State Party to this Convention which is not a party to those treaties.

Article 16

1. Any dispute between two or more States Parties concerning the interpretation or application of this Convention which is not settled by negotiation shall, at the request of one of them, be submitted to arbitration. If within six months from the date of the request for arbitration the parties are unable to agree on the organization of the arbitration, any one of those parties may refer the dispute to the International Court of Justice by request in conformity with the Statute of the Court.

2. Each State may at the time of signature or ratification of this Convention or accession thereto declare that it does not consider itself bound by paragraph 1 of this article. The other States Parties shall not be bound by paragraph 1 of this article with respect to any State Party which has made such a reservation.

3. Any State Party which has made a reservation in accordance with paragraph 2 of this article may at any time withdraw that reservation by notification to the Secretary-General of the United Nations.

Article 17

1. This Convention is open for signature by all States until 31 December 1980 at United Nations Headquarters in New York.

2. This Convention is subject to ratification. The instruments of ratification shall be deposited with the Secretary-General of the United Nations.

3. This Convention is open for accession by any State. The instruments of accession shall be deposited with the Secretary-General of the United Nations.

Article 18

1. This Convention shall enter into force on the thirtieth day following the date of deposit of the twenty-second instrument of ratification or accession with the Secretary-General of the United Nations.

2. For each State ratifying or acceding to the Convention after the deposit of the twenty-second instrument of ratification or accession, the Convention shall enter into force on the thirtieth day after deposit by such State of its instrument of ratification or accession.

Article 19

1. Any State Party may denounce this Convention by written notification to the Secretary-General of the United Nations.

2. Denunciation shall take effect one year following the date on which notification is received by the Secretary-General of the United Nations.

Article 20

The original of this Convention, of which the Arabic, Chinese, English, French, Russian and Spanish texts are equally authentic, shall be deposited with the Secretary-General of the United Nations, who shall send certified copies thereof to all States.

IN WITNESS WHEREOF, the undersigned, being duly authorized thereto by their respective Governments, have signed this Convention, opened for signature at New York on 18 December 1979.

I hereby certify that the foregoing text is a true copy of the International Convention against the taking of hostages, adopted by the General Assembly of the United Nations on 17 December 1979, the original of which is deposited with the Secretary-General of the United Nations.

For the Secretary-General: The Legal Counsel
United Nations, New York, March 24, 1980.

International Convention Against The Taking of Hostages
State Which Are Parties*

Antigua
Barbuda
Bahamas, The
Barbados
Bhutan
Canada
Chile 1
Dominica
Egypt
El Salvador 2
Finland
Germany, Fed. Rep. 3
Guatemala
Honduras
Iceland
Italy
Jordan
Kenya 2
Korea
Lesotho
Malawi
Mauritius
Mexico
New Zealand 4
Norway
Panama
Philippines

Portugal
Spain
Suriname
Sweden
Switzerland
Togo
Trinidad & Tobago
Union of Sov. Soc. Rep.
United Kingdom 5
United States
Yugoslavia

Notes:
   1 With declaration.
   2 With reservation.
   3 Applicable to Berlin (West).
   4 Applicable to Cook Is. and Niue.
   5 Applicable to territories under the territorial sovereignty of the United Kingdom.

* Information provided by the Department of State, as of June 19, 1987

Document 2

Convention on the Physical Protection of Nuclear Material

The States Parties to This Convention, October 26, 1979

Recognizing the right of all States to develop and apply nuclear energy for peaceful purposes and their legitimate interests in the potential benefits to be derived from the peaceful application of nuclear energy,

Convinced of the need for facilitating international co-operation in the peaceful application of nuclear energy,

Desiring to avert the potential dangers posed by the unlawful taking and use of nuclear material,

Convinced that offences relating to nuclear material are a matter of grave concern and that there is an urgent need to adopt appropriate and effective measures to ensure the prevention, detection and punishment of such offences,

Aware of the Need for international co-operation to establish, in conformity with the national law of each State Party and with this Convention, effective measures for the physical protection of nuclear material,

Convinced that this Convention should facilitate the safe transfer of nuclear material,

Stressing also the importance of the physical protection of nuclear material in domestic use, storage and transport,

Recognizing the importance of effective physical protection of nuclear material used for military purposes, and understanding that such material is and will continue to be accorded stringent physical protection,

Have agreed as follows:

Article 1

For the purposes of this Convention:

(a) "nuclear material" means plutonium except that with isotopic concentration exceeding 80% in plutonium-238; uranium-233; uranium enriched in the isotopes 235 or 233; uranium containing the mixture of isotopes as occurring in nature other than in the form of ore or ore-residue; any material containing one or more of the foregoing;

(b) "uranium enriched in the 235 or 233" means uranium containing the isotopes 235 or 233 or both in an amount such that the abundance ratio of the sum of these isotopes to the isotope 238 is greater than the ratio of the isotope 235 to the isotope 238 occurring in nature;

(c) "international nuclear transport" means the carriage of a consignment of nuclear material by any means of transportation intended to go beyond the territory of the State where shipment originates beginning with the departure from a facility of the shipper in that State and ending with the arrival at a facility of the receiver within the State of ultimate destination.

Article 2

1. The Convention shall apply to nuclear material used for peacful purposes while in international nuclear transport.

2. With the exception of articles 3 and 4 and paragraph 3 of article 5, this Convention shall also apply to nuclear material used for peaceful purposes while in domestic use, storage and transport.

3. Apart from the commitments expressly undertaken by States Parties in the articles covered by paragraph 2 with respect to nuclear material used for peaceful purposes while in domestic use, storage and transport, nothing in this Convention shall be interpreted as affecting the sovereign rights of a State regarding the domestic use, storage and transport of such nuclear material.

Article 3

Each State Party shall take appropriate steps within the framework of its national law and consistent with international law to ensure as far as practicable that, during international nuclear transport, nuclear material within its territory, or on board a ship or aircraft under its jurisdiction insofar as such ship or aircraft is engaged in the transport to or from that State, is protected at the levels described in Annex I.

Article 4

1. Each State Party shall not export or authorize the export of nuclear material unless the State Party has received assurances that such material will be protected during the international nuclear transport at the levels described in Annex I.

2. Each State Party shall not import or authorize the import of nuclear material from a State not party to this Convention unless the State Party has received assurances that such material will during the international nuclear transport be protected at the levels described in Annex I.

3. A State Party shall not allow the transit of its territory by land or internal waterways or through its airports or seaports of nuclear material between States that are not parties to this Convention unless the State Party has received assurances as far as practicable that this nuclear material will be protected during international nuclear transport at the levels described in Annex I.

4. Each State Party shall apply within the framework of its national law the levels of physical protection described in Annex I to nuclear material being transported from a part of that State to another part of the same State through international waters or airspace.

5. The State Party responsible for receiving assurances that the nuclear material will be protected at the levels described in Annex I according to paragraphs 1 to 3 shall identify and inform in advance States which the nuclear material is expected to transit by land or internal waterways, or whose airports or seaports it is expected to enter.

6. The responsibility for obtaining assurances referred to in paragraph 1 may be transferred by mutual agreement, to the State Party involved in the transport as the importing State.

7. Nothing in this article shall be interpreted as in any way affecting the territorial sovereignty and jurisdiction of a State, including that over its airspace and territorial sea.

Article 5

1. States Parties shall identify and make known to each other directly or through the International Atomic Energy Agency their central authority and point of contact having responsibility for physical protection of nuclear material and for co-ordinating recovery and response operations in the event of any unauthorized removal, use or alteration of nuclear material or in the event of credible threat thereof.

2. In the case of theft, robbery or any other unlawful taking of nuclear material or of credible threat thereof, States Parties shall, in accordance with their national law, provide co-operation and assistance to the maximum feasible extent in the recovery and protection of such material to any State that so requests. In particular:

(a) a State Party shall take appropriate steps to inform as soon as possible other States, which appear to it to be concerned, of any theft, robbery or other unlawful taking of nuclear material or credible threat thereof and to inform, where appropriate, international organizations;

(b) as appropriate, the States Parties concerned shall exchange information with each other or international organizations with a view to protecting threatened nuclear material, verifying the integrity of the shipping container, or recovering unlawfully taken nuclear material and shall:

(i) co-ordinate their efforts through diplomatic and other agreed channels;

(ii) render assistance, if requested;

(iii) ensure the return of nuclear material stolen or missing as a consequence of the above-mentioned events.

The means of implementation of this co-operation shall be determined by the States Parties concerned.

3. States Parties shall co-operate and consult as appropriate, with each other directly or through international organizations, with a view to obtaining guidance on the design, maintenance and improvement of systems of physical protection of nuclear material in international transport.

Article 6

1. States Parties shall take appropriate measures consistent with their national law to protect the confidentiality of any information which they receive in confidence by virtue of the provisions of this Convention from another State Party or through participation in an activity carried out for the implementation of this Convention. If State Parties provide information to international organizations in confidence, steps shall be taken to ensure that the confidentiality of such information is protected.

2. State Parties shall not be required by this Convention to provide any information which they are not permitted to communicate pursuant to national law or which would jeopardize the security of the State concerned or the physical protection of nuclear material.

Article 7

1. The intentional commission of:

(a) an act without lawful authority which constitutes the receipt, possession, use, transfer, alteration, disposal or dispersal of nuclear material and which causes or is likely to cause death or serious injury to any person or substantial damage to property;

(b) a theft or robbery of nuclear material;

(c) an embezzlement or fraudulent obtaining of nuclear material;

(d) an act constituting a demand for nuclear material by threat or use of force or by any other form of intimidation;

(e) a threat:

(i) to use nuclear material to cause death or serious injury to any person or substantial property damage, or

(ii) to commit an offense described in subparagraph (b) in order to compel a natural or legal person, international organization or State to do or to refrain from doing any act;

(f) an attempt to commit any offense described in paragraphs (a), (b) or (c); and

(g) an act which constitutes participation in any offense described in paragraphs (a) to (f)

shall be made a punishable offense by each State Party under its national law.

2. Each State Party shall make the offenses described in this article punishable by appropriate penalties which take into account their grave nature.

Article 8

1. Each State Party shall take such measures as may be necessary to establish its jurisdiction over the offenses set forth in article 7 in the following cases:

(a) when the offense is committed in the territory of that State or on board a ship or aircraft registered in that State;

(b) when the alleged offender is a national of that State.

2. Each State Party shall likewise take such measures as may be necessary to establish its jurisdiction over these offenses in cases where the alleged offender is present in its territory and it does not extradite him pursuant to article 11 to any of the States mentioned in paragraph 1.

3. This Convention does not exclude any criminal jurisdiction exercised in accordance with national law.

4. In addition to the State Parties mentioned in paragraphs 1 and 2, each State Party may, consistent with international law, establish its jurisdiction over the offenses set forth in article 7 when it is involved in international nuclear transport as the exporting or importing State.

Article 9

Upon being satisfied that the circumstances so warrant, the State Party in whose territory the alleged offender is present shall take appropriate measures, including detention, under its national law to ensure his presence for the purpose of prosecution or extradition. Measures taken according to this article shall be notified without delay to the States required to establish jurisdiction pursuant to article 8 and, where appropriate, all other States concerned.

Article 10

The State Party in whose territory the alleged offender is present shall, if it does not extradite him, submit, without exception whatsoever and without undue delay, the case to its competent authorities for the purpose of prosecution, through proceedings in accordance with the laws of that State.

Article 11

1. The offences in article 7 shall be deemed to be included as extraditable offences in any extradition treaty existing between States Parties. States Parties undertake to include those offences as extraditable offenses in every future extradition treaty to be concluded between them.

2. If a State Party which makes extradition conditional on the existence of a treaty receives a request for extradition from another State Party with which it has no extradition treaty, it may at its option consider this Convention as the legal basis for extradition in respect of those offences. Extradition shall be subject to the other conditions provided by the law of the requested State.

3. States Parties which do not make extradition conditional on the existence of a treaty shall recognize those offences as extraditable offences between themselves subject to the conditions provided by the law of the requested State.

4. Each of the offences shall be treated, for the purpose of extradition between States Parties, as if it had been committed not only in the place in which it occurred but also in the territories of the States Parties required to establish their jurisdiction in accordance with paragraph 1 of article 8.

Article 12

Any person regarding whom proceedings are being carried out in connection with any of the offenses set forth in article 7 shall be guaranteed fair treatment at all stages of the proceedings.

Article 13

1. States Parties shall afford one another the greatest measure of assistance in connection with criminal proceedings brought in respect of the offenses set forth in article 7, including the supply of evidence at their disposal necessary for the proceedings. The law of the State requested shall apply in all cases.

2. The provisions of paragraph 1 shall not affect obligations under any other treaty, bilateral or multilateral, which governs or will govern, in whole or in part, mutual assistance in criminal matters.

Article 14

1. Each State Party shall inform the depositary of its laws and regulations which give effect to this Convention. The depositary shall communicate such information periodically to all States Parties.

2. The State Party where an alleged offender is prosecuted shall, wherever practicable, first communicate the final outcome of the proceed-

ings to the States directly concerned. The State Party shall also communicate the final outcome to the depositary who shall inform all States.

3. Where an offence involves nuclear material used for peaceful purposes in domestic use, storage or transport, and both the alleged offender and the nuclear material remain in the territory of the State Party in which the offence was committed, nothing in this Convention shall be interpreted as requiring that State Party to provide information concerning criminal proceedings arising out of such an offense.

Article 15

The Annexes constitute an integral part of this Convention.

Article 16

1. A conference of States Parties shall be convened by the depositary five years after the entry into force of this Convention to review the implementation of the Convention and its adequacy as concerns the preamble, the whole of the operative part and the annexes in the light of the then prevailing situation.

2. At intervals of not less than five years thereafter, the majority of States Parties may obtain by submitting a proposal to this effect to the depositary, the convening of further conferences with the same object.

Article 17

1. In the event of a dispute between two or more States Parties concerning the interpretation of application of this Convention, such States Parties shall consult with a view to the settlement of the dispute by negotiation, or by any other peaceful means of setting disputes acceptable to all parties to the dispute.

2. Any dispute of this character which cannot be settled in the manner prescribed in paragraph 1 shall, at the request of any party to such dispute, be submitted to arbitration or referred to the International Court of Justice for decision. Where a dispute is submitted to arbitration, if, within six months from the date of the request, the parties to the dispute are unable to agree on the organization of the arbitration, a party may request the President of the International Court of Justice or the Secretary-General of the United Nations to appoint one or more arbitrators. In case of conflicting requests by the parties to the dispute, the request to the Secretary-General of the United Nations shall have priority.

3. Each State Party may at the time of signature, ratification, acceptance or approval of this Convention or accession thereto declare that it does not consider itself bound by either or both of the dispute settlement procedures provided for in paragraph 2. The other States Parties shall not be bound by a dispute settlement procedure provided for in paragraph 2, with respect to a State Party which has made a reservation to that procedure.

4. Any State Party which has made a reservation in accordance with paragraph 3 may at any time withdraw that reservation by notification to the depositary.

Article 18

1. This Convention shall be open for signature by all States at the Headquarters of the International Atomic Energy Agency in Vienna and at the Headquarters of the United Nations in New York from 3 March 1980 until its entry into force.

2. This Convention is subject to ratification, acceptance or approval by the signatory States.

3. After its entry into force, this Convention will be open for accession by all States.

4. (a) This Convention shall be open for signature or accession by international organizations and regional organizations of an integration or other nature, provided that any such organization is constituted by sovereign States and has competence in respect of the negotiation, conclusion and application of international agreements in matters covered by this Convention.

(b) In matters within their competence, such organizations shall, on their own behalf, exercise the rights and fulfill the responsibilities which this Convention attributes to States Parties.

(c) When becoming party to this Convention such an organization shall communicate to the depositary a declaration indicating which States are members thereof and which articles of this Convention do not apply to it.

(d) Such an organization shall not hold any vote additional to those of its Member States.

5. Instruments of ratification, acceptance, approval or accession shall be deposited with the depositary.

Article 19

1. This Convention shall enter into force on the thirtieth day following the date of deposit of the twenty first instrument of ratification, acceptance or approval with the depositary.

2. For each State ratifying, accepting, approving or acceding to the Convention after the date of deposit of the twenty first instrument of ratification, acceptance or approval, the Convention shall enter into force on the thirtieth day after the deposit by such State of its instrument of ratification, acceptance, approval or accession.

Article 20

1. Without prejudice to article 16 a State Party may propose amendments to this Convention. The proposed amendment shall be submitted to the depositary who shall circulate it immediately to all States Parties. If a majority of States Parties request the depositary to convene a conference to consider the proposed amendments, the depositary shall invite all States Parties to attend such a conference to begin not sooner than thirty days after the invitations are issued. Any amendment adopted at the conference by a two-thirds majority of all States Parties shall be promptly circulated by the depositary to all States Parties.

2. The amendment shall enter into force for each State Party that deposits its instrument of ratification, acceptance or approval of the amendment on

the thirtieth day after the date on which two thirds of the States Parties have deposited their instruments of ratification, acceptance or approval with the depositary. Thereafter, the amendment shall enter into force for any other State Party on the day on which that State Party deposits its instrument of ratification, acceptance or approval of the amendment.

Article 21

1. Any State Party may denounce this Convention by written notification to the depositary.

2. Denunciation shall take effect one hundred and eighty days following the date on which notification is received by the depositary.

Article 22

The depositary shall promptly notify all States of:

(a) each signature of this Convention;

(b) each deposit of an instrument of ratification, acceptance, approval or accession;

(c) any reservation or withdrawal in accordance with article 17;

(d) any communication made by an organization in accordance with paragraph 4 (c) of article 18;

(e) the entry into force of this Convention

(f) the entry into force of any amendment to this Convertion; and

(g) any denunciation made under article 21.

Article 23

The original of this Convention, of which the Arabic, Chinese, English, French, Russian and Spanish texts are equally authentic, shall be deposited with the Director General of the International Atomic Energy Agency who shall send certified copies thereof to all States.

Annex I

Levels of Physical Protection to be Applied in International Transport of Nuclear Material as Categorized in Annex II

1. Levels of physical protection for nuclear material during storage incidental to international nuclear transport include:

(a) For Category III materials, storage within an area to which access is controlled;

(b) For Category II materials, storage within an area under constant surveillance by guards or electronic devices, surrounded by a physical barrier with a limited number of points of entry under appropriate control or any area with an equivalent level of physical protection;

(c) For Category I material, storage within a protected area as defined for Category II above, to which, in addition, access is restricted to persons whose trustworthiness has been determined, and which is under surveillance by guards who are in close communication with appropriate response forces. Specific measures taken in this context should have as their object the detection and prevention of any assault, unauthorized access or unauthorized removal of material.

2. Levels of physical protection for nuclear material during international transport include:

(a) For Category II and III materials, transportation shall take place under special precautions including prior arrangements among sender, receiver, and carrier, and prior agreement between natural or legal persons subject to the jurisdiction and regulation of exporting and importing States, specifying time, place and procedures for transferring transport responsibility;

(b) For Category I materials, transportation shall take place under special precautions identified above for transportation of Category II and III materials, and in addition, under constant surveillance by escorts and under conditions which assure close communication with appropriate response forces;

(c) For natural uranium other than in the form of ore or ore-residue, transportation protection for quantities exceeding 500 kilograms U shall include advance notification of shipment specifying mode of transport, expected time of arrival and confirmation of receipt of shipment.

IN WITNESS WHEREOF, the undersigned, being duly authorized, have signed this Convention, opened for signature at Vienna and at New York on 3 March 1980.

Annex II
Table: Categorization of Nuclear Material

Material	Form	Category I	Category II	Category III*
1. Plutonium[1]	Unirradiated[2]	2 kg or more	Less than 2 kg but more than 500 g.	500 g or less but more than 15 g.
2. Uranium-235	Unirradiated[2]:			
	—uranium enriched to 20% U^{235} or more	5 kg or more	Less than 5 kg but more than 1 kg.	1 kg or less but more than 15 g.
	—uranium enriched to 10% U^{235} but less than 20%		10 kg or more	Less than 10 kg but more than 1 kg.
	—uranium enriched above natural, but less than 10% U^{235}.			10 kg or more.

Material	Form	Category		
		I	II	III*
3. Uranium-233 ... Unirradiated[2]		2 kg or more..	Less than 2 kg but more than 500 g.	500 g or less but more than 15 g.
4. Irradiated fuel			Depleted or natural uranium, thorium or low-enriched fuel (less than 10% fissile content).[45]	

[1]All plutonium except that with isotopic concentration exceeding 80% in plutonium-238.

[2]Material not irradiated in a reactor or material irradiated in a reactor but with a radiation level equal to or less than 100 rads/hour at one metre unshielded.

[3]Quantities not falling in Category III and natural uranium should be protected in accordance with prudent management practice.

[4]Although this level of protection is recommended, it would be open to States, upon evaluation of the specific circumstances, to assign a different category of physical protection.

[5]Other fuel which by virtue of its original fissile material content is classified as Category I and II before irradiation may be reduced one category level while the radiation level from the fuel exceeds 100 rads/hour at one metre unshielded.

Document 3

Excerpts, Summit Conference Statements

Bonn: Joint Statement on International Terrorism, July 17, 1978 (From *Public Papers of the Presidents,* Jimmy Carter, 1978). Bonn Economic Summit Conference. *Joint Statement on International Terrorism. July 17, 1978.*

The heads of state and government, concerned about terrorism and the taking of hostages, declare that their governments will intensify their joint efforts to combat international terrorism.

To this end, in cases where a country refuses extradition or prosecution of those who have hijacked an aircraft and/or do not return such aircraft, the heads of state and government are jointly resolved that their governments should take immediate action to cease all flights to that country.

At the same time, their governments will initiate action to halt all incoming flights from the country or from any country by the airlines of the country concerned. The heads of state and government urge other governments to join them in this commitment.

Tokyo: Joint Statement on Hijacking, read as part of Prime Minister Ohira's remarks to reporters at the conclusion of the conference, June 29, 1979 (From *Public Papers of the Presidents,* Jimmy Carter, 1979). Tokyo Economic Summit Conference. *Remarks to Reporters at the Conclusion of the Conference. June 29, 1979.*

Prime Minister Ohira. Now then, I would like to open the joint press conference. . . .

Further, in the present summit, following up on what was taken up in the last summit in Bonn, we adopted a statement on air hijacking, which I will now read.

"All the heads of state and government"—excuse me, I take it back; I have the wrong text in front of me. [*Laughter*]

This is concerning the statement. At the request of heads of state and government who participated in the summit, I, in my capacity of chairman of the meeting, am pleased to make the following statement which concerns the declaration of air hijacking issued in Bonn in July 1978. I now read the statement.

"The heads of state and government express their pleasure with the broad support expressed by other states for the declaration of hijacking made at the Bonn Summit in July 1978.

"They noted that procedures for the prompt implementation of the

---

*Chancellor Helmut Schmidt read the joint statement during his remarks at the Bonn Stadt theater at the conclusion of the Bonn Economic Summit Conference.

declaration have been agreed upon and that to date enforcement measures under the declaration have not been necessary.

"They also noted with satisfaction the widespread adherence to the conventions dealing with unlawful interference with international civil aviation. Extensive support for these conventions and the Bonn declaration on hijacking reflects the acceptance by the international community as a whole of the principles expressed therein."

Venice: Statement on the Taking of Diplomatic Hostages, June 22, 1980 and Statement on Hijacking, June 22, 1980 (From *Public Papers of the Presidents,* Jimmy Carter, 1980). Venice Economic Summit Conference. *Statement on the Taking of Diplomatic Hostages. June 22, 1980.*

Gravely concerned by recent incidents of terrorism involving the taking of hostages and attacks on diplomatic and consular premises and personnel, the Heads of State and Government reaffirm their determination to deter and combat such acts. They note the completion of work on the International Convention Against the Taking of Hostages and call on all States to consider becoming parties to it as well as to the Convention on the Prevention and Punishment of Crimes Against Internationally Protected Persons of 1973.

The Heads of State and Government vigorously condemn the taking of hostages and the seizure of diplomatic and consular premises and personnel in contravention of the basic norms of international law and practice. The Heads of State and Government consider necessary that all Governments should adopt policies which will contribute to the attainment of this goal and to take appropriate measures to deny terrorists any benefits from such criminal acts. They also resolve to provide to one another's diplomatic and consular missions support and assistance in situations involving the seizure of diplomatic and consular establishments or personnel.

The Heads of State and Government recall that every State has the duty under international law to refrain from organizing, instigating, assisting or participating in terrorist acts in another State or acquiescing in organised activities within its territory directed towards the commission of such acts, and deplore in the strongest terms any breach of this duty.

Venice Economic Summit Conference. *Statement on Hijacking. June 22, 1980.*

The Heads of State and Government expressed their satisfaction at the broad support of the international community for the principles set out in the Bonn Declaration of July 1978 as well as in the international Conventions dealing with unlawful interference with civil aviation. The increasing adherence to these Conventions and the responsible attitude taken by States with respect to air-hijacking reflect the fact that these principles are being accepted by the international community as a whole.

The Heads of State and Government emphaisze that hijacking remains a threat to international civil aviation and that there can be no relaxation of efforts to combat this threat. To this end they look forward to continuing cooperation with all other Governments.

Ottawa: Statement on Terrorism, July 20, 1981 (From *Public Papers of the Presidents,* Ronald Reagan, 1981). Ottawa Economic Summit Conference Statement on Terrorism. *July 20, 1981.*

1. The Heads of State and Government, seriously concerned about the active support given to international terrorism through the supply of money and arms to terrorist groups, and about the sanctuary and training offered terrorists, as well as the continuation of acts of violence and terrorism such as aircraft hijacking, hostage-taking and attacks against diplomatic and consular personnel and premises, reaffirm their determination vigorously to combat such flagrant violations of international law. Emphasizing that all countries are threatened by acts of terrorism in disregard of fundamental human rights, they resolve to strengthen and broaden action within the international community to prevent and punish such acts.

2. The Heads of State and Government view with particular concern the recent hijacking incidents which threaten the safety of international civil aviation. They recall and reaffirm the principles set forth in the 1978 Bonn Declaration and note that there are several hijackings which have not been resolved by certain states in conformity with their obligations under international law. They call upon the governments concerned to discharge their obligations promptly and thereby contribute to the safety of international civil aviation.

3. The Heads of State and Government are convinced that, in the case of the hijacking of a Pakistan International Airlines aircraft in March, the conduct of the Babrak Karmal government of Afghanistan, both during the incident and subsequently in giving refuge to the hijackers, was and is in flagrant breach of its international obligations under the Hague Convention to which Afghanistan is a party, and constitutes a serious threat to air safety. Consequently the Heads of State and Government propose to suspend all flights to and from Afghanistan in implementation of the Bonn Declaration unless Afghanistan immediately takes steps to comply with its obligations. Furthermore, they call upon all states which share their concern for air safety to take appropriate action to persuade Afghanistan to honour its obligations.

4. Recalling the Venice Statement on the Taking of Diplomatic Hostages, the Heads of State and Government approve continued cooperation in the event of attacks on diplomatic and consular establishments or personnel of any of their governments. They undertake that in the event of such incidents, their governments will immediately consult on an appropriate response. Moreover, they resolve that any state which directly aids and abets the commission of terrorist acts condemned in the Venice Statement, should face a prompt international response. It was agreed to exchange information on terrorist threats and activities, and to explore cooperative measures for dealing with and countering acts of terrorism, for promoting more effective implementation of existing anti-terrorist conventions, and for securing wider adherence to them.

London: Declaration on International Terrorism, June 9, 1984 (From the *Public Papers of the Presidents,* Ronald Reagan, 1984). London Economic Summit Conference Declaration on International Terrorism. *June 9, 1984.*

1. The Heads of State and Government discussed the problem of international terrorism.

2. They noted that hijacking and kidnapping had declined since the Declarations of Bonn (1978), Venice (1980) and Ottawa (1981) as a result of improved security measures, but that terrorism had developed other techniques, sometimes in association with traffic in drugs.

3. They expressed their resolve to combat the threat by every possible means, strengthening existing measures and developing effective new ones.

4. They were disturbed to note the ease with which terrorists move across international boundaries, and gain access to weapons, explosives, training and finance.

5. They viewed with serious concern the increasing involvement of states and governments in acts of terrorism, including the abuse of diplomatic immunity. They acknowledged the inviolability of diplomatic missions and other requirements of international law; but they emphasised the obligations which that law also entails.

6. Proposals which found support in the discussion included the following:

— closer co-operation and co-ordination between police and security organisations and other relevant authorities, especially in the exchange of information, intelligence and technical knowledge;

— scrutiny by each country of gaps in its national legislation which might be exploited by terrorists;

— use of the powers of the receiving state under the Vienna Convention in such matters as the size of diplomatic missions, and the number of buildings enjoying diplomatic immunity;

— action by each country to review the sale of weapons to states supporting terrorism;

— consultation and as far as possible cooperation over the expulsion or exclusion from their countries of known terrorists, including persons of diplomatic status involved in terrorism.

7. The Heads of State and Government recognised that this is a problem which affects all civilised states. They resolved to promote action through competent international organisations and among the international community as a whole to prevent and punish terrorist acts.

Tokyo: Statement on International Terrorism, May 5, 1986 (From *Weekly Compilation of Presidential Documents,* Monday, May 12, 1986, Vol. 22, No. 19). Tokyo Economic Summit. *Statement on International Terrorism. May 5, 1986.*

1. We, the Heads of State or Government of seven major democracies and the representatives of the European Community, assembled here in Tokyo,

strongly reaffirm our condemnation of international terrorism in all its forms, of its accomplices and of those, including governments, who sponsor or support it. We abhor the increase in the level of such terrorism since our last meeting, and in particular its blatant and cynical use as an instrument of government policy. Terrorism has no justification. It spreads only by the use of contemptible means, ignoring the values of human life, freedom and dignity. It must be fought relentlessly and without compromise.

2. Recognizing that the continuing fight against terrorism is a task which the international community as a whole has to undertake, we pledge ourselves to make maximum efforts to fight against that scourge. Terrorism must be fought effectively through determined, tenacious, discreet and patient action combining national measures with international cooperation. Therefore, we urge all like-minded nations to collaborate with us, particularly in such international fora as the United Nations, the International Civil Aviation Organization and the International Maritime Organization, drawing on their expertise to improve and extend countermeasures against terrorism and those who sponsor or support it.

3. We, the Heads of State or Government, agree to intensify the exchange of information in relevant fora on threats and potential threats emanating from terrorist activities and those who sponsor or support them, and on ways to prevent them.

4. We specify the following as measures open to any government concerned to deny to international terrorists the opportunity and the means to carry out their aims, and to identify and deter those who perpetrate such terrorism. We have decided to apply these measures within the framework of international law and in our own jurisdictions in respect of any state which is clearly involved in sponsoring or supporting international terrorism, and in particular of Libya, until such time as the state concerned abandons its complicity in, or support for, such terrorism. These measures are:

— refusal to export arms to states which sponsor or support terrorism;

— strict limits on the size of the diplomatic and consular missions and other official bodies abroad of states which engage in such activities, control of travel of members of such missions and bodies, and, where appropriate, radical reductions in, or even the closure of, such missions and bodies;

— denial of entry to all persons, including diplomatic personnel, who have been expelled or excluded from one of our states on suspicion of involvement in international terrorism or who have been convicted of such a terrorist offence;

— improved extradition procedures within due process of domestic law for bringing to trial those who have perpetrated such acts of terrorism;

— stricter immigration and visa requirements and procedures in respect of nationals of states which sponsor or support terrorism:

— the closest possible bilateral and multilateral cooperation between police and security organizations and other relevant authorities in the fight against terrorism.

Each of us is committed to work in the appropriate international bodies to which we belong to ensure that similar measures are accepted and acted upon by as many other governments as possible.

5. We will maintain close cooperation in furthering the objectives of this statement and in considering further measures. We agree to make the 1978 Bonn Declaration more effective in dealing with all forms of terrorism affecting civil aviation. We are ready to promote bilaterally and multilaterally further actions to be taken in international organizations or fora competent to fight against international terrorism in any of its forms.

Venice: Statement on Terrorism, June 9, 1987 (From "Venice Statements on East-West Relations, Terrorism and Persian Gulf," *New York Times,* June 10, 1987).

Terrorism

We, the heads of state or government of seven major democracies and the representatives of the European Community assembled here in Venice, profoundly aware of our peoples' concern at the threat posed by terrorism:

— Reaffirm our commitment to the statements on terrorism made at previous summits, in Bonn, Venice, Ottawa, London and Tokyo;

— Resolutely condemn all forms of terrorism, including aircraft hijackings and hostage-taking, and reiterate our belief that whatever its motives, terrorism has no justification;

— Confirm the commitment of each of us to the principle of making no concessions to terrorists or their sponsors;

— Remain resolved to apply, in respect of any state clearly involved in sponsoring or supporting international terrorism, effective measures within the framework of international law and in our own jurisdictions;

— Welcome the progress made in international cooperation against terrorism since we last met in Tokyo in May 1986, and in particular the initiative taken by France and Germany to convene in May in Paris a meeting of ministers of nine countries, who are responsible for counterterrorism;

— Reaffirm our determination to combat terrorism both through national measures and through international cooperation among ourselves and with others, when appropriate, and therefore renew our appeal to all like-minded countries to consolidate and extend international cooperation in all appropriate fora;

— Will continue our efforts to improve the safety of travelers. We welcome improvements in airport and maritime security, and encourage the work of I.C.A.O. and I.M.O. in this regard. Each of us will continue to monitor closely the activities of airlines which raise security problems. The heads of state or government have decided on measures, annexed to this statement, to make the 1978 Bonn Declaration more effective in dealing with all forms of terrorism affecting civil aviation;

— Commit ourselves to support the rule of law in bringing terrorists to justice. Each of us pledges increased cooperation in the relavant fora and within the framework of domestic and international law on the investigation, apprehension and prosecution of terrorists. In particular we reaffirm the principle established by relevant international conventions of trying or extraditing, according to national laws and those international conventions, those who have perpetrated acts of terrorism.

Annex

The heads of state or government recall that in their Tokyo statement on international terrorism they agreed to make the 1978 Bonn Declaration more effective in dealing with all forms of terrorism affecting civil aviation. To this end, in cases where a country refuses extradition or prosecution of those who have committed offenses described in the Montreal Convention for the Suppression of Unlawful Acts against the Safety of Civil Aviation and/or does not return the aircraft involved, the heads of state or government are jointly resolved that their Governments shall take immediate action to cease flights to that country as stated in the Bonn Declaration.

At the same time, their governments will initiate action to halt incoming flights from that country or from any country by the airlines of the country concerned as stated in the Bonn Declaration.

The heads of state or government intend also to extend the Bonn Declaration in due time to cover any future relevant amendment to the above convention or any other aviation conventions relating to the extradition or prosecution of the offenders.

The heads of state or government urge other governments to join them in this commitment.

Document 4

Excerpt, Concluding Document of the Vienna Meeting 1986 of Representatives of the Participating States of the Conference on Security and Co-operation in Europe, Held on the Basis of the Provisions of the Final Act Relating to the Follow-up to the Conference

8. The participating states unreservedly condemn, as criminal, all acts, methods and ·practices of terrorism, wherever and by whomever committed, including those which jeopardize friendly relations among States and their security, and agree that terrorism cannot be justified under any circumstances.

9. They express their determination to work for the eradication of terrorism both bilaterally and through multilateral co-operation, particularly in such international fora as the United Nations, the International Civil Aviation Organization and the International Maritime Organization and in accordance with the relevant provisions of the Final Act and the Madrid Concluding Document.

10. Convinced of the need to combine measures at a national level with reinforced international cooperation, the participating States express their intention

(a) to pursue a policy of firmness in response to terrorist demands;

(b) to reinforce and develop bilateral and multilateral co-operation among themselves in order to prevent and combat terrorism as well as to increase efficiency in existing co-operation at the bilateral level or in the framework of groups of States, including, as appropriate, through the exchange of information;

(c) to prevent on their territories illegal activities of persons, groups or organizations that instigate, organize or engage in the perpetration of acts of terrorism or subversive or other activities directed towards the violent overthrow of the regime of another participating State;

(d) to take effective measures for the prevention and suppression of acts of terrorism directed at diplomatic or consular representatives and against terrorism involving violations of the Vienna Conventions on Diplomatic and Consular Relations, in particular their provisions relating to diplomatic and consular privileges and immunities;

(e) to ensure the extradition or prosecution of persons implicated in terrorist acts and to cooperate closely in cases of conflict of jurisdiction where several States are concerned, acting in both respects in accordance with the relevant international agreements;

(f) to consider becoming parties, if they have not yet done so, to the relevant international conventions relating to the suppression of acts of terrorism;

(g) to continue to work in the appropriate international bodies in order to improve and extend measures against terrorism and to ensure that the relevant agreements are accepted and acted upon by as many States as possible.

Document 5

Recommendations of American and Soviet Participants in U.S.-Soviet meetings on preventing terrorism held in Moscow January 23-27, 1989, and sponsored by *Literaturnaya Gazeta* and Search for Common Ground

In their bilateral relations, as well as their respective relations with all other states, the United States and the Soviet Union should recognize their strong mutual interest in preventing acts of violence, especially acts of terrorism, whatever their motivation, which could lead to larger conflicts.

We, the participants of this meeting, recognize that the most serious threats of terrorism involve:

- terrorist incidents that could provoke nuclear confrontation;
- terrorist incidents that could provoke warfare or armed conflict;
- terrorist incidents that could involve mass casualties, including nuclear, chemical or biological incidents.

We further recognize that the most likely threats of terrorism involve an array of common terrorist tactics that affect both the US and USSR and include:

- attacks on civil aviation including the sabotage of aircraft and hijacking of aircraft;
- attacks on ships and platforms and the mining of sea lanes;
- attacks on internationally recognized protected persons (e.g. diplomats, children).

Therefore, the United States and the Soviet Union should work together in a manner consistent with general principles of international law to prevent terrorism and control its consequences where it occurs. The issue of international terrorism—its causes, manifestations and consequences—should be high on their bilateral agenda.

In consideration thereof, the participants in the meeting recommend to our respective governments:

1. The creation of a standing bilateral group and channel of communications for the exchange of information pertinent to terrorism. This would provide a designated link for conveying requests and relaying information during a crisis created by a terrorist incident.

2. The provision of mutual assistance, (information, diplomatic assistance, technical assistance, etc.), when requested, in the investigation or resolution of terrorist incidents.

3. The prohibition of the sale or transfer of military explosives and certain classes of weapons (to be designated in bilateral discussion between the Soviet and American governments) to non-government organizations; and the restriction and increased controls on the sale or transfer of military explosives and the same classes of weapons to states.

4. The initiation of bilateral discussions to explore the utility of requiring the addition of chemical or other types of "tags" to commercial and military explosives to make them more easily detectable and to aid in the investigation of terrorist bombings.

5. The initiation of joint efforts to prevent terrorists from acquiring chemical, biological, nuclear, or other means of mass destruction. (For

example, the 1980 Vienna Convention on the Protection of Nuclear Material.)

6. Consistent with the national security interests as defined by each nation, the exchange of technology that may be useful in preventing or combatting terrorism.

7. The conduct of joint exercises and simulations for the purpose of exploring and developing further means of Soviet-American cooperation during terrorist threats or incidents.

8. In order to strengthen implementation of existing antiterrorism conventions:

(a) The US and the USSR should establish a bilateral group to review the effectiveness of these conventions as instruments for the apprehension, prosecution and punishment of persons who commit the crimes, covered by the Conventions.

(b) The US and the USSR should jointly or individually initiate efforts toward the UN Security Council establishing a Standing Committee on International Terrorism to perform a similar function on a multilateral basis.

9. In order to fill the gaps that exist in current international law and institutions regarding international terrorism:

(a) The US and the USSR should propose the drafting of an international convention that would cover threats and acts of violence that deliberately target the civilian population and that have an international dimension.

(b) The Security Council Standing Committee on International Terrorism referred to above in 8 (b) should study and recommend to the Security Council effective measures to ensure that neither military nuclear weapons nor nuclear material designed for civilian use ever get in the hands of terrorists.

(c) Disputes concerning the interpretation and application of the antiterrorist conventions should, if not settled by other means, be referred to the International Court of Justice for resolution.

(d) Renewed consideration should be given to the feasibility of an international tribunal—either *ad hoc* or having a permanent status—to try persons accused of acts of international terrorism.

ABOUT THE AUTHOR

Dr. Martha Crenshaw was an American Scholar-in-Residence at the Institute for East-West Security Studies in 1987–1988. A specialist on international terrorism, Dr. Crenshaw is currently Professor of Government at Wesleyan University. In 1977–1978 she was a Fellow at the Richardson Institute for Conflict and Peace Research in London. Dr. Crenshaw has also served as a consultant to the U.S. secretary of state.